Slimming World's

four seasons
cookbook

Slimming World's
four seasons cookbook

120 recipes to take you through the year

EBURY
PRESS

Published in 2008 by Ebury Press, an imprint of Ebury Publishing
Ebury Publishing is a division of the Random House Group

The Random House Group Limited Reg. No. 954009
Addresses for companies within the Random House Group
can be found at www.randomhouse.co.uk

A CIP catalogue record for this book is available from the British Library.

ISBN 9780091922405

Recipes created by Sunil Vijayakar
Editor: Patricia Burgess
Designer: Nicky Barneby

Food photography: Jon Whitaker
Food stylist: Sunil Vijayakar
Prop stylist: Rachel Jukes

For Slimming World
Founder and chairman: Margaret Miles-Bramwell
Managing director: Caryl Richards
Project coordinators: Allison Brentnall and Beverley Farnsworth
Text by Christine Michael

The Random House Group makes every effort to ensure that the papers
used in our books are made from trees that have been legally sourced
from well-managed and credibly certified forests. Our paper procurement
policy can be found on www.randomhouse.co.uk

Printed and bound in Singapore by Tien Wah Press Ltd

To buy books by your favourite authors and register for offers visit www.rbooks.co.uk

cookery
notes

- Both metric and imperial measures are given for the recipes. Follow either set of measures as they are not interchangeable.
- All spoon measures are level: 1 tsp = 5ml spoon, 1 tbsp = 15ml spoon.
- Ⓥ Suitable for vegetarians
- ❄ Suitable for freezing
- Ovens should be preheated to the specified temperature. Grills should also be preheated.
- Use large eggs unless otherwise specified.
- Note that some of the recipes contain lightly cooked eggs. Avoid serving these to anyone who is pregnant or in a vulnerable health group, as there is a small risk of salmonella infection.
- Always use fresh herbs, unless dried herbs are suggested in the recipe.
- Use freshly ground black pepper and sea salt unless otherwise specified.

foreword

Dear Reader

A very warm welcome to the *Four Seasons Cookbook*, the latest collection of wonderfully tasty and deliciously healthy recipes from Slimming World.

At a time when there are so many scare stories about what we should and shouldn't eat, it's a real pleasure to bring you a book that's a celebration of the very best of fresh, seasonal food that we can all enjoy to the full.

And as someone who understands from personal, painful experience how hard it can be to love food and manage your weight successfully, it's an even greater joy to know that all these recipes can help you slim, as they're based on Free Foods, the secret at the heart of Food Optimising, Slimming World's phenomenal eating plan.

By basing meals on healthy, filling, delicious Free Foods, Food Optimisers discover they can lose weight without ever feeling deprived, hungry or guilty – the three enemies of successful slimming. Feeling that you are not just given permission to eat, but actually encouraged to eat (and then to eat a bit more!) is what sets Food Optimising apart from other slimming diets. No more do we have to give up our favourite foods, eating with our family or having a social life – sacrifices that are counter-productive because they feel more like punishments. Gone too is the additional burden of low self-esteem, which can make us feel we somehow don't deserve the simple pleasures in life that naturally slim people take for granted.

When I launched Slimming World 39 years ago, my burning passion was to show that losing weight doesn't have to be about denying yourself pleasures, making sacrifices and carrying burdens – the very opposite, in fact! Within a warm, friendly Slimming World group, members discover that it's normal to have an appetite, and normal to love good food – and that it's so freeing to eat to satisfy your appetite instead of following what the 'diet rules' say. And Slimming World understands that you have a life too! Food Optimising fits in easily with social life, working life, family life – however you choose to live it and enjoy it to the max.

Belonging to a Slimming World group opens up a whole world of compassionate, constructive support, both from fellow members and from your Consultant, who has not only had top-class training, but also knows from personal experience exactly how it feels to have a weight problem.

Week by week, as they set their own goals, plan their strategies for success and overcome obstacles, members learn that we can 'make our own weather'. Having a laugh with your group and basking in the warmth of their support can be enough to brighten up the bleakest day and help restore your faith in yourself because you are a confident, competent person who can choose your own next step to success. It's not surprising that many members describe Slimming World as a ray of sunshine in their week!

As Slimming World's founder, it's such a privilege to meet successful members who are thrilled to have escaped that demoralising cycle of 'diet at New Year, fail by Easter', and found a healthy lifestyle that makes it easy for them to enjoy good food, stay slim all year round, and never, ever go hungry. As this *Four Seasons Cookbook* shows, the perfect time to start your weight-loss journey is now, whatever the weather or the time of year. And, of course, Slimming World's door is open all year round, and there's always a smile and a warm welcome waiting for you. We do hope we'll see you there soon. Together we really can discover the amazing you!

With warmest wishes

Margaret Miles-Bramwell, FRSA
Founder and Chairman

introduction

We all look forward to seasonal celebrations through the year, and many of them are associated with food. Easter, Hallowe'en, Bonfire Night and Christmas are just some of the milestones that we mark each year with special meals or foods.

But how many of us take that spirit of celebration into our kitchens every day by making the most of the glorious fresh produce that each season has to offer? We may have our particular 'special occasion' favourites, such as satsumas at Christmas, strawberries in June or apples and pears in the autumn, but the rest of the year we may be fairly unadventurous with the range of fresh fruit, vegetables, meat and fish that we buy.

Yet the truth is that there are many great reasons for widening our food horizons – especially if our priority is to eat healthily and manage our weight.

The first is that by basing meals on fresh foods, we know what's on our plate and can control how much fat, sugar or salt we add, which is essential when we want to eat healthily, and not always possible when we rely on ready-made meals and processed foods.

Nutritionists also advise us to 'eat a rainbow' of brightly coloured fruit and veg to ensure that our diet is rich in vitamins and minerals; and eating what's fresh and in season makes this a pleasure. After all, which would you rather have:

a vitamin pill or a ripe, red tomato, a juicy orange and a crisp green apple?

Fresh food is terrific value too: a whole basketful of fresh vegetables can cost less than the price of a single-portion ready meal. And bagging a bargain is also the perfect opportunity to get the family excited about food and engaged in healthy eating, whether you're harvesting your own home-grown veg, enjoying a trip to a pick-your-own farm, or filling your basket at the local market.

Following the seasons with our menus also means more variety in our food, helping to keep boredom at bay, which can be the undoing of all our plans to eat healthily. Getting into a 'food rut' is all too easy when we stick to the same route around the supermarket every week, increasing the temptation to break out of our self-imposed food straitjacket.

And maybe most important of all is the sheer explosion of taste and flavour we can experience by enjoying fresh foods in season. Now that so much imported produce is available in supermarkets all year round, it's easy to forget the taste sensation of the first English strawberries of the summer, the first fragrant Scottish raspberries, the warm, heady scent of local tomatoes, or the earthy, nutty taste of freshly lifted new potatoes.

If you've picked up the *Four Seasons Cookbook* to help you lose weight, you might wonder why we're focusing so much on delicious food! Isn't thinking about food all day just going to make it even harder to reach your target weight?

The answer, if you're losing weight the Slimming World way, is: absolutely not! That's because Slimming World's Food Optimising plan is all about enjoying generous, tasty, everyday meals that make the very most of what each season has to offer.

The secret of Food Optimising is Free Foods – a huge list of foods you can enjoy as much as you like, whenever you like, and still be confident that you'll lose weight each week. And we don't mean 'diet foods' that have no flavour or filling power! As well as all fresh fruit and vegetables, Free Foods include lean meat and fish, pasta, potatoes, pulses, eggs and very low fat dairy products – so there's no chance you'll be eating just a big salad or a heap of steamed vegetables!

With 124 recipes all based on Free Foods, the *Four Seasons Cookbook* shows you how to incorporate the finest and tastiest seasonal foods into meals that family and friends will love all year round, and that you'll be able to enjoy to the full along with everyone else – including going back for seconds if you like.

If you haven't yet discovered Food Optimising, these delicious recipes may well whet your appetite to find out more about losing weight the Slimming World way. To read more about the science behind Food Optimising, turn to page 182.

Yet Food Optimising is just one element of the Slimming World experience: in the *Four Seasons Cookbook* you can also learn more about how Slimming World helps hundreds of thousands of people each year to lose weight and improve their health, energy and self-confidence. In the warm, friendly, supportive surroundings of a

Slimming World group, members learn and share all kinds of tips and techniques to help make their slimming journey a success, with plenty of praise, laughter and fun along the way.

If you're already a Slimming World member, we hope that the *Four Seasons Cookbook* inspires you with lots more Food Optimising ways to celebrate seasonal food in your meals each week.

And if you haven't yet joined us, we hope you'll feel that Slimming World is the place where you can start your voyage of discovery to a new love of food and a new slim, healthy you.

Now that would definitely be a cause for celebration, whatever the time of year!

For details of a warm and friendly group near you, call 0844 897 8000 or visit **www.slimmingworld.com**

free food
storecupboard

All these ingredients are used in the recipes in this book and are Free Foods for both Green and Original choices, unless otherwise stated.

CANS AND BOTTLES
Artificial sweetener
Butter beans (Green choice only)
Cannellini beans (Green choice only)
Capers
Mixed beans (Green choice only)
Red kidney beans (Green choice only)
Sweetcorn (Green choice only)
Tomatoes, chopped (plain and with herbs)

FROM THE FRIDGE
Chillies, bird's-eye, green and red
Eggs
Fresh herbs, e.g.
    basil
    bay leaf
    chervil
    chives
    coriander
    dill
    lemongrass
    mint
    oregano
    parsley (standard and flat-leaf)
    rosemary
    sage
    tarragon
    thyme
Garlic
Ginger, fresh root
Lemons and limes
Onions (red and white) and shallots
Quark soft cheese
Tomatoes, all kinds
Very low fat natural fromage frais
Very low fat natural yogurt

STAPLES

Bovril stock, beef and chicken

Bulgur wheat (Green choice only)

Celery salt

Couscous (Green choice only)

Dried herbs and spices, whole or ground, e.g.

   allspice

   black onion seeds (kalonji/nigella)

   caraway seeds

   cardamom seeds

   cayenne

   chilli powder (mild, medium and hot)

   Chinese five-spice

   cinnamon (ground and sticks)

   cloves

   coriander (ground and seeds)

   cumin (ground and seeds)

   curry powder (mild, medium and hot)

   dried bay leaves

   fennel seeds

   ground ginger

   ground star anise

   herbes de Provence

   mixed dried herbs: all varieties

   mustard seeds (black and yellow)

   nutmeg

   oregano

   paprika (mild, hot and sweet smoked)

   peppercorns (black, mixed and pink)

   pimenton (mild paprika)

   saffron threads

   thyme

   turmeric

   vanilla pods

Dried red chilli flakes

Fat-free dressings, French-style and vinaigrette

Fish sauce

Fry Light

Garlic salt

Gelatine

Lentils, all varieties (Green choice only)

Mustard powder

Passata (sieved tomatoes)

Pasta and egg noodles, all types, dried
   (Green choice only)

Polenta (fine and coarse) (Green choice only)

Rice noodles (Green choice only)

Rice, all varieties: e.g. Arborio, basmati, brown,
   long grain, risotto (Green choice only)

Sea salt

Soy sauces (dark and light)

Tabasco sauce

Vanilla essence/extract

Vecon

Vinegars: e.g. red wine, sherry and
   white wine

Worcestershire sauce

spring

WHAT'S IN SEASON

baby beetroot ~ baby spinach ~ chicken
crab ~ new potatoes ~ purple sprouting broccoli ~
rhubarb ~ skate ~ spring greens ~ spring lamb

spring vegetable soup

The beauty of this soup is that you can use any seasonal vegetables of your choice, so it's always different.

SERVES 4 Ⓥ ❄
EASY
Syns per serving
Original: Free
Green: Free

Preparation time 5 minutes
Cooking time about 15 minutes

Fry Light

8 spring onions, finely chopped

2 sticks celery, finely chopped

2 garlic cloves, peeled and finely chopped

1 litre/1¾ pints water or vegetable stock made with Vecon

400g/14oz diced spring vegetables, such as baby spinach leaves, leeks, baby carrots

salt and freshly ground black pepper

To garnish

chopped fresh herbs

1. Spray a non-stick saucepan with Fry Light and place over a medium heat. Add the spring onions, celery and garlic and stir-fry for 2–3 minutes.

2. Add the water or stock and the vegetables, bring to the boil and season well. Reduce the heat to medium and cook for 10–12 minutes.

3. Serve immediately, garnished with chopped fresh herbs.

watercress and baby leaf spinach soup

Watercress is a robustly flavoured salad leaf with a wonderful peppery taste, and it's also very nutritious.

SERVES 4 Ⓥ ❋
EXTRA EASY
Syns per serving
Green: Free
Original: 1½

Preparation time 6–8 minutes
Cooking time about 15 minutes

Fry Light

4 leeks, white parts only, very thinly sliced

2 garlic cloves, peeled and finely chopped

1 large potato, peeled and cut into 1cm/½in dice

110g/4oz watercress, finely chopped

110g/4oz baby leaf spinach

1.5 litres/2½ pints water or vegetable stock made with Vecon

salt and freshly ground black pepper

To serve
very low fat natural fromage frais

1. Spray a non-stick saucepan with Fry Light and place over a medium heat. Add the leeks, garlic and potato and stir-fry for 2–3 minutes.

2. Add the watercress, spinach and water or stock and bring to the boil. Cover and cook gently for 10–12 minutes, or until the potatoes are tender. Season well.

3. Using a hand-held electric blender or a food processor, blend the soup until smooth. Serve ladled into warmed bowls with a swirl of fromage frais.

Baby spinach
Spring cooks find baby spinach wonderfully versatile because it's just as tasty eaten raw in salads, such as our Bean and Baby Spinach Salad (page 27), as it is in this flavour-packed Watercress and Baby Leaf Spinach Soup. Its dark green leaves contain many beneficial plant compounds, including lutein (which can help eye health), and minerals such as folate and potassium.

prawn, pink grapefruit
and watercress salad

The sharp flavour of grapefruit marries well with shellfish. You can use regular yellow grapefruit in place of the pink if you wish.

SERVES 4

EASY

Syns per serving
Original: Free
Green: 7

Preparation time 15 minutes

500g/1lb 2oz cooked and peeled tiger prawns

1 large pink grapefruit, peeled and cut into segments

2 red onions, peeled, halved and thinly sliced

200g/7oz cherry tomatoes, halved

110g/4oz watercress

For the dressing

4 tbsp fat-free salad dressing

1 tsp mustard powder

1 tsp artificial sweetener

2 tbsp white wine vinegar

1 garlic clove, peeled and crushed

salt and freshly ground black pepper

1. Place the prawns, grapefruit, onions, tomatoes and watercress in a wide salad bowl.

2. Put all the dressing ingredients in a clean, screw-top jar, season well and shake vigorously.

3. Pour the dressing over the salad ingredients, toss well to mix and serve immediately.

orange, red onion
and black olive salad

The flavours of the orange, red onion and olives complement each other very well in this simple refreshing salad.

SERVES 4 ⓥ
EXTRA EASY
Syns per serving
Original: 2
Green: 2

Preparation time 15 minutes

4 large oranges

2 red onions, peeled

14 pitted black olives

a small handful of mint leaves

1 tbsp sherry vinegar

1 tbsp olive oil

salt and freshly ground black pepper

1. Slice off the top and bottom of the oranges, then cut off the peel and pith with a sharp knife. Cut the oranges into slices 1cm/½in thick and arrange on a serving plate.

2. Cut the onions into thin rings and arrange over the orange slices.

3. Scatter over the olives and mint leaves, drizzle with the vinegar and olive oil, season well and serve.

baked egg timbales

These dense and flavoursome little mushroom and egg cakes can be made ahead of time, and eaten hot or at room temperature.

SERVES 4 Ⓥ ❋
WORTH THE EFFORT
Syns per serving
Original: 3
Green: 3

Preparation time 10 minutes
Cooking time about 1 hour

Fry Light
6 spring onions, finely sliced
1 red chilli, deseeded and finely chopped
300g/11oz baby button mushrooms, finely chopped
1 garlic clove, peeled and finely chopped
salt and freshly ground black pepper
6 tbsp finely chopped dill
25g/1oz fine dried wholemeal breadcrumbs
4 medium eggs
4 tbsp very low fat natural fromage frais
4 tbsp finely grated Parmesan cheese

To serve
crisp green salad

1. Spray a large frying pan with Fry Light and place over a medium heat. Add the spring onions and chilli and stir-fry for 1–2 minutes. Add the mushrooms to the pan along with the garlic. Cook for about 15–20 minutes, stirring often, until the mushrooms are lightly browned and any liquid released has evaporated. Remove from the heat, season well and stir in the dill.

2. Preheat the oven to 180°C/Gas 4. Spray 4 x 200ml non-stick timbale moulds with Fry Light and line the bases with discs of non-stick baking parchment. Coat the sides with the breadcrumbs, discarding any excess.

3. Lightly beat the eggs with the fromage frais and Parmesan. Season and stir into the mushroom mixture. Spoon this into the prepared moulds, place in a baking dish and pour in enough boiling water to come halfway up the sides of the moulds. Bake for 35–40 minutes, or until firm.

4. Remove from the oven and allow to rest for 10 minutes. Run the tip of a knife around the edge of the timbales and turn out onto individual plates. Serve with a crisp green salad.

baby beetroot
and little gem salad

Sweet and delicious baby beetroot comes into season right now. Use larger beetroot if you want: just cut them into slices or bite-sized cubes when cooked and peeled.

SERVES 4 Ⓥ
EXTRA EASY
Syns per serving
Original: Free
Green: Free

Preparation time 10 minutes
Cooking time 30 minutes

500g/1lb 2oz baby beetroot, trimmed

2 baby gem lettuces, leaves separated, washed and dried

200g/7oz red radishes, thinly sliced

4 tbsp chopped chives

For the dressing
8 tbsp fat-free salad dressing
2 tbsp finely diced shallots

1. Boil the beetroots in a large pan of water for 30 minutes, or until tender when pierced with a sharp knife. Drain and peel. Cut into halves or slices and place in a serving dish.

2. Add the lettuce and radishes to the cooked beetroot and toss to combine.

3. Mix together the dressing and the shallots, then pour over the beetroot mixture and toss well. Scatter over the chives and serve immediately.

new potato and apple salad

This salad would work well as a starter, light lunch or a meal accompaniment. That's what you call versatile!

SERVES 4 Ⓥ

EASY

Syns per serving

Green: 2

Original: 9

Preparation time 15–20 minutes

800g/1lb 12oz new potatoes

2 red apples, cut into bite-sized pieces

3 sticks celery, finely sliced

6 spring onions, finely sliced

8 tbsp finely chopped dill

4 tbsp finely snipped chives

For the dressing

8 tbsp Hellmann's Extra Light Mayonnaise

3 tbsp wine vinegar

1 tsp runny honey

1 tbsp Dijon or wholegrain mustard

salt and freshly ground black pepper

1. Cut the potatoes into halves or bite-sized pieces and boil in lightly salted water until tender. Drain and place in a large mixing bowl with the apple, celery, spring onion, dill and chives.

2. Mix together all the dressing ingredients, season well and pour over the potato mixture. Toss well and serve warm or at room temperature.

New potatoes

With their earthy, wholesome taste and waxy, creamy texture, hot new potatoes are the perfect accompaniment to grilled meat or fish, and they're sensational served cold with a tangy dressing, as in our New Potato and Apple Salad. Vitamin C and potassium make new potatoes a healthy choice as well as a family favourite. Don't forget to leave the skins on to maximise the fibre.

chilli corn bread

Polenta is another name for coarse-ground cornmeal. We've used it to make this delicious 'bread', which would be a great lunch if served with a crisp green salad.

SERVES 4 Ⓥ ❄

EASY

Syns per serving

Green: Free

Original: 12½

Preparation time 15 minutes

Cooking time 35–40 minutes

Fry Light

250g/9oz fine polenta

1 tsp baking powder

salt and freshly ground black pepper

4 large eggs, lightly beaten

300g/11oz very low fat natural yogurt

275g/10oz canned sweetcorn kernels, drained

2 mild green chillies, deseeded and finely chopped

200g/7oz bottled roasted red peppers in brine, rinsed, drained and finely chopped

6 spring onions, finely sliced

1. Preheat the oven to 170°C/Gas 3. Spray a 20cm/8in cast-iron skillet or an ovenproof, non-stick baking tin with Fry Light.

2. Mix together the polenta and baking powder. Season well.

3. In a jug, combine the beaten egg and yogurt and pour into the polenta mixture. Add the sweetcorn, chillies, red peppers and spring onions and stir lightly to combine.

4. Pour the batter into the prepared skillet or tin and bake in the oven for 35–40 minutes, until firm and lightly browned on top. Cut the warm bread into squares or slices and serve immediately.

stir-fried purple sprouting
broccoli with noodles

Broccoli is great stir-fried, and helps make this dish a winning combination of colours, textures and flavours!

SERVES 4 Ⓥ

EASY

Syns per serving
Green: Free
Original: 15

Preparation time 10 minutes
Cooking time 15 minutes

350g/12oz dried medium egg noodles

Fry Light

1 mild red chilli, finely sliced

4 garlic cloves, peeled and finely sliced

1 tsp finely grated ginger

2 tbsp very finely diced lemongrass

400g/14oz purple sprouting broccoli, thick stems halved

6 tbsp light soy sauce

salt and freshly ground black pepper

1. Cook the noodles according to the packet instructions, then drain and keep warm.

2. Meanwhile, spray a large non-stick wok or frying pan with Fry Light and place over a high heat. Add all the ingredients, excluding the soy sauce, and stir-fry for 6–8 minutes.

3. Stir in the soy with 3–4 tablespoons of water.

4. Add the drained noodles and continue to stir and cook over a high heat for 3–4 minutes, or until the broccoli is just tender. Season well and serve immediately.

> **Purple sprouting broccoli**
> Besides being a beautiful colour, purple sprouting broccoli is even tastier and more packed with vitamins and minerals than its green cousin. British-grown varieties, available in early spring, can be lightly steamed or boiled (like asparagus spears), or served in a stir-fry, such as this Stir-fried Purple Sprouting Broccoli with Noodles.

bean and baby spinach salad

A simple salad that's made even easier by using canned beans. If you prefer to use dried beans, you will need 150g/5oz for this recipe. Soak them overnight in cold water and then cook them for approximately 1–1½ hours.

SERVES 4

EXTRA EASY

Syns per serving

Green: 1

Original: 5

Preparation time 15 minutes

1 x 410g can cannellini beans, rinsed and drained

200g/7oz baby spinach leaves

1 red onion, peeled, halved and thinly sliced

2 plum tomatoes, roughly chopped

For the dressing

1 garlic clove, peeled and finely grated

1 tsp ground coriander

1 tsp cayenne

6 tbsp Kraft Light Caesar Dressing

2 tbsp very low fat natural yogurt

1. Mix together all the dressing ingredients, then set aside.

2. Place the beans, spinach, onion and tomatoes in a wide, shallow salad bowl. Pour over the dressing and toss well before serving.

crab, papaya and mint salad

Buying fresh crabmeat from the fishmonger can be expensive, so you could use crabmeat canned in brine as an alternative. Just remember to drain it first.

SERVES 4

EXTRA EASY

Syns per serving

Original: ½

Green: 4½

Preparation time 20 minutes

300g/11oz ripe papaya flesh, finely sliced

1 small cucumber, halved and very thinly sliced

300g/11oz fresh white crabmeat, cooked

a small handful of mint leaves

For the dressing

1 tbsp finely diced stem ginger

4 tbsp white wine vinegar

3 tbsp fat-free vinaigrette or French-style salad dressing

1 tsp artificial sweetener

1 red chilli, finely diced

salt and freshly ground black pepper

1. First make the dressing by whisking all the ingredients together in a bowl until combined. Season well.

2. In a shallow salad bowl, gently toss the papaya and cucumber together with the dressing.

3. Divide this mixture between 4 salad plates and top with the crab. Sprinkle over the mint leaves and serve immediately.

Crab

May is the peak season for fresh British crabs: the rich brown body meat and sweet white leg meat are both highly prized, and sources of B vitamins and minerals. Crab is traditionally served in salads and in teatime sandwiches, but it also loves zingy flavours, as in our Crab, Papaya and Mint Salad.

vegetable
rice noodles

Rice noodles work best in this recipe, but you could change them for egg noodles, if you prefer. Just cook them according to the packet instructions.

SERVES 4 Ⓥ

WORTH THE EFFORT

Syns per serving
Green: Free
Original: 11½

Preparation time 15 minutes
Cooking time 15 minutes

2 garlic cloves, peeled and crushed

1 tsp finely chopped ginger

1 red chilli, deseeded and finely chopped

1 red onion, peeled and finely diced

90ml/3fl oz vegetable stock made with Vecon

2 tbsp dark soy sauce

¼ tsp artificial sweetener (optional)

200g/7oz broccoli florets

200g/7oz mangetout, thinly sliced

250g/9oz bean sprouts

250g/9oz dried medium or thin rice noodles

1 egg, lightly beaten

To serve

sliced spring onion

coriander leaves

lime juice

1. Place the garlic, ginger, chilli, onion, stock, soy and sweetener, if using, in a large non-stick frying pan. Heat through gently for 4–5 minutes.

2. Turn the heat to high and add the vegetables. Stir-fry for 4–5 minutes until the vegetables are just tender.

3. Prepare the noodles according to the packet instructions, then drain and add to the vegetable mixture over a high heat.

4. Lower the heat, then drizzle over the beaten egg, mix well and cook for 1–2 minutes, until the egg is just cooked through.

5. Remove the pan from the heat and divide the noodles between 4 plates. Sprinkle over the spring onion, coriander and a squeeze of lime juice before serving.

beetroot pesto pasta

Raw beetroot can be either boiled or roasted. You can, however, buy cooked fresh beetroot in vacuum packs from most good supermarkets. Don't be tempted to use the ones that are bottled as they are full of vinegar.

SERVES 4 Ⓥ

WORTH THE EFFORT

Syns per serving

Green: Free

Original: 15

Preparation time 5 minutes

Cooking time about 15 minutes

350g/12oz dried fettuccini, tagliatelle or pappardelle (or any other pasta of your choice)

Fry Light

1 red chilli, deseeded and finely chopped

2 tsp cumin seeds

1 tsp fennel seeds

2 tsp crushed coriander seeds

300g/11oz cooked beetroot, very finely chopped

6 spring onions, finely sliced

a small handful of chopped mint and coriander leaves

salt and freshly ground black pepper

1. Cook the pasta according to the packet instructions, then drain and keep warm.

2. While the pasta is cooking, spray a non-stick frying pan with Fry Light and place over a medium heat. Add the chilli and the cumin, fennel and coriander seeds, and stir-fry for 1–2 minutes. Add the beetroot, then stir and cook for 2–3 minutes until warmed through.

3. Add the drained pasta to the beetroot mixture and toss carefully. Remove from the heat, stir in the spring onions and chopped herbs, season well and serve immediately.

> **Beetroot**
> This root vegetable has been eaten since Roman times. It contains valuable supplies of nutrients and is said to be a good source of folate, a type of B vitamin. It can be eaten raw or cooked, as here, in our Beetroot Pesto Pasta recipe, or in gloriously colourful Borscht soup (page 142).

spring vegetable risotto

Arborio is one of the best-known risotto rices. Unlike the long-grain varieties, it has a comparatively plump grain, which becomes creamy when cooked.

SERVES 4 ✱

WORTH THE EFFORT

Syns per serving

With Parmesan

Green: 1

Original: 12

Without Parmesan

Green: Free

Original: 11½

Preparation time 20 minutes

Cooking time about 30 minutes

Fry Light

8–10 spring onions, finely chopped

2 garlic cloves, peeled and finely chopped

6 baby leeks, finely sliced

250g/9oz Arborio or risotto rice

900ml/1½ pints boiling water, or chicken stock made with Bovril

200g/7oz baby carrots, roughly chopped or sliced

200g/7oz baby courgettes, roughly chopped or sliced

salt and freshly ground black pepper

6 tbsp chopped flat-leaf parsley

1 tbsp chopped tarragon

To serve

2 tbsp grated Parmesan cheese (optional)

1. Spray a large, non-stick frying pan with Fry Light and place over a medium heat. Add the spring onions, garlic and leeks and stir-fry for 3–4 minutes.

2. Add the rice and stir-fry for 2–3 minutes. Add a ladleful of the boiling water or stock, then stir and cook until the liquid is absorbed. Repeat, adding a ladleful at a time, until half the stock is used up.

3. Stir in the carrots and courgettes, and continue adding the water or stock as before until it is all used up. The rice should be creamy and al dente (tender, but still retaining a bite). This should take about 20–25 minutes.

4. Remove from the heat, season well and stir in the chopped herbs. Serve ladled into warmed pasta bowls, sprinkled with Parmesan, if using, and eat immediately.

spring green and lentil pilaff

This dish is a great way of using up any leftover rice you may have. It makes a wonderful main course meal too!

SERVES 4 Ⓥ ❄
WORTH THE EFFORT
Syns per serving
Green: Free
Original: 10

Preparation time 20 minutes
Cooking time 30 minutes

110g/4oz Puy or green lentils
Fry Light
2 garlic cloves, peeled and finely diced
1 red onion, peeled, halved and thinly sliced
300g/11oz cherry tomatoes, halved
2 sticks celery, cut into small dice
2 carrots, peeled and cut into small dice
150g/5oz spring greens, finely shredded
350g/12oz cooked long grain rice
a large bunch of flat-leaf parsley, finely chopped
2 tbsp finely chopped mint leaves
salt and freshly ground black pepper

To serve
4 poached eggs (optional)

1. Place the lentils in a large saucepan of lightly salted water and bring to the boil. Reduce the heat and cook gently for 15–20 minutes, or until the lentils are just tender. Drain and keep warm.

2. While the lentils are cooking, spray a large non-stick frying pan with Fry Light and place over a medium heat. Add the garlic and onion and cook for 2–3 minutes, or until softened.

3. Add the tomatoes, celery, carrots and spring greens to the pan and stir-fry for 6–8 minutes, or until the mixture is warmed through and the vegetables are just softened.

4. Add the lentils, rice and herbs to the vegetable mixture and season well. Mix thoroughly and stir-fry for 4–5 minutes. Ladle onto 4 warmed plates and serve immediately, topped with a poached egg, if desired.

Spring greens
Eaten young, spring greens are more delicate in texture and flavour than cabbage, their winter relative. They have a loose head with a pale yellow-green heart, and can be prepared in a variety of ways. They are delicious simply sliced, steamed and served with butter, and they're equally good when added to dishes such as our Spring Green and Lentil Pilaff.

cucumber
and tomato couscous

This light and refreshing salad is perfect for warm summer eating, and makes a great picnic dish. It can be prepared ahead of time and chilled until needed.

SERVES 4 Ⓥ

EASY

Syns per serving

Green: ½

Original: 9

Preparation time 20 minutes

200g/7oz couscous

200g/7oz cherry tomatoes, halved

1 large cucumber, roughly chopped

1 red pepper, deseeded and finely diced

1 yellow pepper, deseeded and finely diced

a large handful of chopped flat-leaf parsley

a small handful of roughly chopped mint leaves

1 red chilli, deseeded and finely chopped

For the dressing

juice of 1 orange

6 tbsp fat-free vinaigrette or French-style salad dressing

1 tsp garlic salt

1 tsp celery salt

1. Place the couscous in a large, heatproof bowl and pour over enough boiling water to just cover. Place a plate over the bowl and leave for 10–15 minutes.

2. Place the tomatoes, cucumber, peppers, herbs and chilli in a salad bowl.

3. When the couscous has absorbed all the water, fluff up the grains with a fork and add to the salad bowl.

4. Combine all the dressing ingredients in a jug. Pour over the salad and toss well. Serve at room temperature.

pan-cooked skate with bacon

If you cannot get hold of small skate wings, buy two large ones and cut them in half. This dish would be great served with new potatoes in their skins (1 Syn per 25g/1oz boiled on Original).

SERVES 4

WORTH THE EFFORT

Syns per serving
Original: 2
Green: 14

Preparation time 15 minutes
Cooking time 20 minutes

12 lean bacon rashers

4 small skate wings (about 175g/6oz each)

2 tbsp plain flour

1 tsp paprika

1 tsp turmeric

1 tsp ground cumin

salt and freshly ground black pepper

Fry Light

To garnish
chopped flat-leaf parsley
lemon wedges

1. Preheat the grill until very hot. Place the bacon rashers on a rack and grill for 4–5 minutes, or until crispy and golden. Roughly chop them up and keep warm.

2. Rinse the skate wings under running water, pat dry with kitchen paper and place on a clean work surface.

3. Mix together the flour and spices, season well, then transfer to a small, fine sieve. Dust this mixture lightly and evenly over the fish.

4. Preheat the oven to 200°C/Gas 6. Meanwhile, spray a large, non-stick frying pan with Fry Light and place over a high heat. Add the fish floured side down and cook for about 3–5 minutes on each side until lightly golden (you might need to do this in batches, depending on the size of your pan). Transfer to a non-stick baking sheet and place in the oven for 4–5 minutes.

5. To serve, place the skate wings on warmed plates and scatter over the bacon. Garnish with some chopped parsley and wedges of lemon to squeeze over.

> **Skate**
> Although skate wings are ribbed, the flesh comes away easily, which makes them much easier to eat than bony fish. The flesh has a good texture and is delicate and sweet-tasting. In French cuisine skate wings are usually poached and served with a butter sauce, but we've simply floured and 'fried' them in our recipe for Pan-cooked Skate with Bacon.

creamy spiced prawn curry

This curry is great on its own, or you could serve it with lots of steamed spring greens or Free vegetables of your choice.

SERVES 4

EASY

Syns per serving
Original: Free
Green: 7

Preparation time 8 minutes
Cooking time 20–25 minutes

Fry Light

½ onion, finely chopped

2 garlic cloves, peeled and crushed

1 tsp finely grated ginger

2 tbsp mild or medium curry powder

300g/11oz mangetout, trimmed

250ml/9fl oz passata

1–2 tsp artificial sweetener

100ml/3½fl oz water, or chicken stock made with Bovril

800g/1lb 12oz raw tiger prawns, shelled and deveined

salt and freshly ground black pepper

200g/7oz very low fat natural yogurt, whisked

a large handful of finely chopped coriander leaves

1. Spray a large, non-stick frying pan with Fry Light and place over a high heat. Add the onion, garlic, ginger and curry powder and stir-fry for 2–3 minutes.

2. Stir in the mangetout, passata and sweetener with the water or stock, and bring to the boil. Cook over a medium heat for 15 minutes, stirring occasionally, until the mangetout is tender.

3. Stir in the prawns and cook for 6–8 minutes, or until they turn pink and are cooked through. Season well, remove from the heat and stir in the yogurt and coriander just before serving.

grilled chilli prawns
with papaya and ginger salsa

Have finger bowls of hot water and lemon slices at the ready as you will be using your hands to peel off the shells of the cooked prawns.

SERVES 4

WORTH THE EFFORT

Syns per serving

Original: ½

Green: 2½

Preparation time 10 minutes

Cooking time about 6 minutes

24 large, raw tiger prawns (shell on, heads removed)

6 garlic cloves, peeled and crushed

1 tsp dried chilli flakes

salt and freshly ground black pepper

Fry Light

For the salsa

10 tbsp very finely diced papaya

4 tbsp very finely diced red pepper

1 tbsp very finely diced stem ginger

2 tbsp very finely chopped mint

2 tsp finely grated lemon zest

1. Place the prawns in a large mixing bowl and add the garlic and chilli. Season well and spray with Fry Light. Mix well, using your fingers. Set aside to rest.

2. Mix all the salsa ingredients in a bowl, season well and chill until ready to serve.

3. Place the prawns on a hot griddle pan or barbecue and cook for 2–3 minutes on each side, or until they turn pink and are cooked through. Serve with the salsa.

salmon on wilted spring greens

This would make a great light lunch if served with boiled new potatoes in their skins (1 Syn per 25g/1oz on Original).

SERVES 4

WORTH THE EFFORT

Syns per serving

Original: ½

Green: 13

Preparation time 10 minutes plus marinating

Cooking time 25–30 minutes

4 x 150g/5oz thick salmon fillets, skinned

6 tbsp dark soy sauce

2 tsp ground ginger

2 tsp clear honey

salt and freshly ground black pepper

For the spring greens

200g/7oz spring greens

Fry Light

1 onion, peeled, halved and thinly sliced

3 garlic cloves, peeled and sliced

1. Place the salmon in a shallow dish in a single layer. Mix together the soy, ginger and honey, pour over the fish and toss to coat well. Season with pepper, cover and leave to marinate for about 15 minutes.

2. Roughly shred the spring greens. Spray a large, non-stick wok with Fry Light and place over a medium heat. Add the onion and garlic and stir-fry for 3–4 minutes, or until the onion has softened. Turn the heat to high and add the spring greens. Stir-fry for 5–6 minutes, or until just wilted. Season well, then set aside and keep warm while you cook the fish.

3. Preheat the grill to medium-high. Place the salmon on a rack and grill for 12–15 minutes, or until cooked through.

4. To serve, place the spring greens on 4 warmed plates and top each portion with a piece of the salmon.

pot-roast chicken
with leeks and spring herbs

We've used drumsticks and thighs in this recipe, but you could use any chicken portions you like; just remember to remove the skin first.

SERVES 4 ✸

WORTH THE EFFORT

Syns per serving
Original: 7
Green: 6

Preparation time 20 minutes
Cooking time about 2 hours

Fry Light

4 chicken drumsticks, skinless

4 chicken thighs, skinless

6–8 leeks, cut into 3cm/1¼in pieces

2 large carrots, peeled and cut into large chunks

1 head of garlic, separated but not peeled

800g/1lb 12oz baby new potatoes

600ml/1 pint chicken stock made with Bovril

4–5 sprigs of tarragon

4–5 tbsp finely chopped flat-leaf parsley

salt and freshly ground black pepper

200g/7oz green beans, halved

1. Spray a large heatproof casserole dish with Fry Light and place over a high heat. Add the chicken pieces and cook until lightly browned on all sides.

2. Add the leeks, carrots, garlic, potatoes, stock, tarragon and parsley. Season well and bring to the boil. Reduce the heat to low, cover very tightly with a lid and allow to cook gently for 1½ hours.

3. Add the green beans to the casserole and cook for 10 minutes. Remove from the heat, check the seasoning and serve immediately in warmed shallow bowls.

> **Chicken**
> In the past chicken was an Easter treat (hence 'spring chicken'), but it's now popular all year round because it's so tasty and versatile. It marries well with Italian, Indian, Chinese and Thai flavourings, and with the herbs and garlic in the two delicious dishes on these pages. Chicken meat is a good source of protein, and with the skin removed, it's a low-fat choice too.

40 garlic clove chicken

Don't be scared of the amount of garlic used in this traditional French recipe. It actually becomes a sweet and aromatic paste when roasted in its skin, and flavours the chicken beautifully.

SERVES 4 ❄

EASY

Syns per serving
Original: Free
Green: 10½

Preparation time 10 minutes
Cooking time 1½ hours

1 x 800g/1lb 12oz chicken, skinless and jointed

40 garlic cloves, unpeeled

Fry Light

salt and freshly ground black pepper

1 tbsp dried herbes de Provence

1 fresh bouquet garni (10cm/4in stick celery, 1 bay leaf and a few sprigs of thyme and flat-leaf parsley tied together with string)

100ml/3½fl oz chicken stock made with Bovril

1. Preheat the oven to 170°C/Gas 3. Place the chicken and garlic in a snug-fitting ovenproof casserole dish. Spray generously with Fry Light and season well.

2. Scatter over the dried herbs and place the bouquet garni in the middle. Pour over the stock and cover tightly.

3. Place in the oven and cook for 1½ hours, or until the chicken is meltingly tender. To serve, place the chicken on warmed plates and spread with the garlic, squeezed out of its skin, if you wish.

rosemary rack of lamb
with a watercress sauce

For this recipe you need French-trimmed racks of lamb, which means that all the visible fat is removed, leaving just healthy, lean meat. Most supermarkets sell ready-trimmed racks, but if you can't find any, ask your butcher to prepare one for you.

SERVES 4

WORTH THE EFFORT

Syns per serving
Original: Free
Green: 20

Preparation time 5 minutes plus marinating
Cooking time 18–20 minutes

4 tbsp crushed mixed peppercorns

4 garlic cloves, peeled and crushed

2 tbsp finely chopped rosemary leaves

3 tbsp passata

4 x French-trimmed racks of lamb, each weighing about 275g/10oz

For the green herb sauce

110g/4oz watercress, roughly chopped

300g/11oz very low fat natural fromage frais

6–8 tbsp chopped fresh herbs, such as mint and parsley

4 tbsp capers, rinsed and chopped

salt and freshly ground black pepper

1. First make the sauce by placing the watercress, fromage frais, chopped herbs and capers in a food processor and processing until smooth. Season well, transfer to a bowl and set aside until ready to serve.

2. Place the peppercorns, garlic, rosemary and passata in a bowl and mix well. Season with salt.

3. Using a small, sharp knife, make deep cuts all over the flesh side of the lamb racks, then place on a non-stick baking sheet. Spread the peppercorn paste all over the lamb and allow to marinate for 2–3 hours, or overnight if time permits.

4. When ready to cook, preheat the oven to 220°C/Gas 7. Roast the racks for 18–20 minutes, or until cooked to your liking. Remove the racks from the oven, cover with foil and allow to rest for 10 minutes. Leave whole or slice into cutlets, and serve with the herb sauce, plus steamed carrots and green beans.

lamb and spinach casserole

Shoulder of lamb is an economical cut of meat that becomes wonderfully tender when slow-cooked. This makes it perfect for stews and casseroles.

SERVES 4 ✻

WORTH THE EFFORT

Syns per serving

Original: 1

Green: 12

Preparation time 20 minutes

Cooking time under 2 hours

Fry Light

600g/1lb 6oz shoulder of lean lamb, boneless and cut into bite-sized pieces

1 onion, peeled and finely chopped

3 garlic cloves, peeled and finely grated

1 tsp ground ginger

2 tsp turmeric

a large pinch of grated nutmeg

1 tsp ground cinnamon

1 tsp paprika

2 tbsp sultanas

1 x 400g can chopped tomatoes

300ml/½ pint stock made with Bovril or Vecon

salt and freshly ground black pepper

400g/14oz baby leaf spinach

To serve

very low fat natural yogurt, whisked (optional)

1. Spray a large, heavy-based saucepan with Fry Light and brown the lamb, in batches, for 3–4 minutes. Remove with a slotted spoon and set aside.

2. Add the onion, garlic, spices and sultanas to the pan and stir-fry for 1–2 minutes. Add the lamb and stir-fry for 2–3 minutes.

3. Pour in the tomatoes and stock, season well and bring to the boil. Reduce the heat to low, cover tightly and simmer gently (using a heat diffuser if possible) for 1½ hours.

4. Add the spinach in batches until it has all wilted, then cover and cook for 10–12 minutes, stirring occasionally. Remove from the heat and serve drizzled with the yogurt, if desired.

roasted leg of lamb
with carrots and onions

A great dish that uses seasonal spring lamb accompanied with baby carrots and onions – what could be simpler?

SERVES 4

WORTH THE EFFORT

Syns per serving
Original: Free
Green: 17

Preparation time 20 minutes
Cooking time about 1¾ hours

Fry Light

1 x 1kg/2lb 4oz leg of lamb, trimmed of all visible fat

300g/11oz baby carrots or Chantenay carrots, scrubbed

2 onions, peeled and cut into thick wedges

2–3 sprigs of rosemary

2 bay leaves

6–8 garlic cloves, unpeeled

salt and freshly ground black pepper

To serve

2–3 tbsp dried mint

1. Preheat the oven to 190°C/Gas 5. Meanwhile, spray a large roasting tin with Fry Light, place over a high heat and brown the lamb on all sides for 4–5 minutes.

2. Place the lamb in the oven and cook for 50 minutes. Add the carrots, onions, rosemary, bay leaves and garlic around the lamb and season well. Return the pan to the oven for another 40–50 minutes, or until the lamb is tender and the vegetables are cooked through.

3. Remove from the oven, cover with foil and allow to rest for 10 minutes before carving. Sprinkle all over with dried mint before serving.

Spring lamb

The lamb that appears in shops from March onwards is young, pink and tender, a good source of protein, B vitamins, zinc and iron. Leg steaks are delicious grilled with the season's new potatoes and baby spinach, or with an exotic spicy marinade. Our one-pot recipe – Roasted Leg of Lamb with Carrots and Onions – is substantial and tasty on a chilly spring day.

spiced baby spinach with new potatoes

The combination of new potatoes and baby spinach is a match made in heaven, and would be great served with steamed rice (2 Syns per 25g/1oz cooked on Original).

SERVES 4 Ⓥ ❋
EASY
Syns per serving
Green: Free
Original: 6½

Preparation time 15 minutes
Cooking time about 30 minutes

Fry Light

2 small red onions, peeled, halved and thinly sliced

2 garlic cloves, peeled and crushed

1 tsp finely grated ginger

2 tbsp medium curry powder

1 x 400g can chopped tomatoes

700g/1lb 8oz baby new potatoes, scrubbed

300ml/11fl oz water, or vegetable stock made with Vecon

200g/7oz baby spinach leaves

salt and freshly ground black pepper

To garnish

very low fat natural yogurt

coriander

1. Spray a large, non-stick frying pan with Fry Light and place over a gentle heat. Add the onions and stir-fry for 3–4 minutes until soft and lightly browned.

2. Turn the heat to high and add the garlic, ginger and curry powder. Stir-fry for 5–6 minutes.

3. Add the tomatoes, potatoes and water or stock and bring to the boil. Reduce the heat and cook for 15–20 minutes, or until the potatoes are tender.

4. Stir in the spinach, season well and cook until heated through. Remove from the heat, then drizzle with the yogurt and garnish with coriander.

garlicky broccoli

A speciality of the Rioja region in Spain, this simple but aromatic dish transforms the humble broccoli into something fresh and exciting. It would work equally well with cauliflower.

SERVES 4 Ⓥ ❄

EASY

Syns per serving
Original: Free
Green: Free

Preparation time 10 minutes
Cooking time under 20 minutes

800g/1lb 12oz broccoli florets
Fry Light
3 garlic cloves, peeled and finely chopped
1 tbsp sweet paprika
2 tbsp white wine vinegar
salt and freshly ground black pepper

To garnish
finely chopped parsley

1. Break the broccoli florets into bite-sized pieces and add to a large saucepan of lightly salted boiling water. Cook for 6–8 minutes, then drain thoroughly and set aside.

2. Spray a large, non-stick frying pan with Fry Light and place over a medium-high heat. Add the garlic and stir-fry for 1–2 minutes. Add the broccoli, paprika and vinegar, season well and cook, stirring, over a high heat for 3–4 minutes.

3. Remove from the heat, sprinkle over the parsley and serve immediately.

celeriac dauphinoise

This is a simple, peasant-style, one-pot dish, originally made with lots of cream. Here we have substituted stock and Quark. To ring the changes you can use potatoes instead of celeriac.

SERVES 4 ❄
EASY
Syns per serving
Original: Free
Green: Free

Preparation time 15 minutes
Cooking time about 1 hour

Fry Light

800g/1lb 12oz celeriac, peeled

2 large onions, peeled, halved and thinly sliced

150g/5oz Quark soft cheese

200ml/7fl oz chicken stock made with Bovril, or vegetable stock made with Vecon

3 tsp garlic salt

freshly ground black pepper

To serve

chopped parsley

steamed green vegetables

1. Preheat the oven to 200°C/Gas 6. Spray a medium ovenproof dish with Fry Light.

2. Cut the celeriac into thin sticks. Arrange half in the prepared dish, then cover with the onions. Top with the remaining celeriac.

3. Beat the Quark until smooth, then stir in the stock and garlic salt to make a smooth mixture. Season well with pepper. Pour this mixture over the vegetables, spray lightly with Fry Light and bake in the oven for 50–60 minutes. (If the top starts browning too quickly, cover with foil.)

4. Remove from the oven and allow the dish to rest for a few minutes before serving. Sprinkle with chopped parsley and serve with steamed Free green vegetables of your choice.

tip

Celeriac is a hard vegetable, so use a very sharp knife to peel it, or heat in the microwave for about 5 minutes on HIGH to soften it slightly before peeling.

ginger rhubarb
with orange custard

The tangy rhubarb and smooth custard complement each other perfectly in this simple dessert.

SERVES 4 Ⓥ ❄
WORTH THE EFFORT

Syns per serving
Original: 4½
Green: 4½

Preparation time 10 minutes
Cooking time 20–25 minutes
plus chilling

600g/1lb 6oz rhubarb, cut into chunks

6–8 tbsp artificial sweetener

2 tsp ground ginger

1 vanilla pod, split in half lengthways

400g/14oz canned low fat custard

finely grated zest of 1 orange

To serve

very low fat natural fromage frais

2 vanilla pods, split in half lengthways

1. Preheat the oven to 180°C/Gas 4. Mix the rhubarb, sweetener, ginger and vanilla pod in an ovenproof dish and place in the oven for 20–25 minutes (depending on the thickness of the rhubarb). Remove from the oven, discard the vanilla pod and leave to cool.

2. Divide the mixture between 4 large dessert glasses and chill in the fridge for 4–5 hours.

3. Mix the custard with most of the orange zest and spoon over the rhubarb mixture. Top each serving with a tablespoon of fromage frais, then sprinkle with the remaining orange zest and decorate with the split vanilla pods. Serve immediately.

Rhubarb

Candy-pink rhubarb stalks look sweet, but taste very tart, so are best poached or stewed with sweetener and spices, as in our Ginger Rhubarb with Orange Custard. Although we eat it as a fruit, rhubarb is actually a vegetable, and a good source of vitamin C and fibre; it's also delicious in crumbles, fools, tarts and compotes.

orange and saffron cake

Saffron has a distinctive and lasting aroma, and imparts a wonderfully rich yellow colour to any dish it's used in.

SERVES 6–8 Ⓥ
EASY
Syns per serving
If serving 6
Original: 6½
Green: 6½

If serving 8
Original: 5
Green: 5

Preparation time 25 minutes
Cooking time 25–30 minutes

4 eggs, separated
3 tsp saffron threads soaked in 3 tbsp warm water
50g/2oz caster sugar
5 tbsp artificial sweetener
150g/5oz self-raising flour
1 tsp baking powder
2 tbsp finely grated orange zest

For the sauce

zest of 2 oranges, cut into long, fine strips
juice of 2 oranges
1 tbsp arrowroot
4 tbsp artificial sweetener

To serve

orange segments
very low fat natural fromage frais

1. Preheat the oven to 190°C/Gas 5. Line a 22cm/8½in cake tin with non-stick baking parchment.

2. Place the egg yolks, saffron mixture, caster sugar, sweetener, flour, baking powder and orange zest in a bowl and whisk until thick and pale.

3. Whisk the egg whites in a separate bowl until softly peaked, then fold into the egg yolk mixture. Spoon into the prepared cake tin and place in the oven for 25–30 minutes, or until the cake is risen and firm to the touch. Remove from the oven and leave in the tin for 10 minutes before turning onto a wire rack to cool.

4. Meanwhile, place the sauce ingredients in a small pan with 60ml/2fl oz of water and bring to the boil, whisking constantly. When the liquid starts to thicken, remove from the heat and leave to cool.

5. To serve, cut the cake into slices and drizzle with the sauce. Accompany each serving with orange segments and a dollop of fromage frais.

mango sorbet

Canned mango purée should be available in larger supermarkets. If you can't find it, buy fresh mango instead (about 400g/14oz) and simply purée it.

SERVES 4 ❋

EASY

Syns per serving

Original: 3

Green: 3

Preparation time about 30 minutes plus freezing

350g/12oz canned mango purée

2–3 tbsp artificial sweetener

1 x 200g pot Müllerlight vanilla yogurt

1. Place all the ingredients in a blender and blend until smooth. Transfer the mixture to a shallow, freezerproof container and leave in the freezer for 2–3 hours, or until the sides and base of the sorbet are starting to freeze, but the centre is still liquid.

2. Stir the mixture with a fork, then return it to the freezer for 4–5 hours, stirring it with a fork every 30–40 minutes. Freeze until firm.

3. Before serving, transfer the sorbet from the freezer to the fridge for 10–15 minutes to soften slightly. Scoop into individual sundae glasses and eat straight away.

tip

To make this sorbet in an ice-cream machine, place the mixture in the drum and churn until thick enough to scoop. Transfer to a freezerproof container and place in the freezer until ready to use.

summer

WHAT'S IN SEASON
asparagus ~ broad beans ~ gooseberries
melon ~ peppers ~ pork ~ squid ~
summer berries ~ sweetcorn ~ tomatoes

raspberry, melon and cucumber salad

The fragrant, sweet-tasting flesh of the Galia melon makes this a refreshing salad that would be a great starter or main meal accompaniment.

SERVES 4 Ⓥ

EXTRA EASY

Syns per serving

Original: Free

Green: Free

Preparation time 10 minutes

1 Galia melon

1 cucumber

200g/7oz raspberries

a small handful of finely chopped dill

6 tbsp fat-free vinaigrette

salt and freshly ground black pepper

1. Quarter the melon, scoop out the seeds and remove the peel. Slice the melon into thin wedges and cut each wedge in half.

2. Peel the cucumber and cut it in half lengthways. Remove the seeds with a teaspoon, then thinly slice the flesh.

3. Place the melon and cucumber in a bowl and mix well. Scatter over the raspberries and dill and drizzle with the dressing. Season and toss well. Serve slightly chilled or at room temperature.

roasted tomato and bulgur salad

This salad is great eaten straight away, when still warm, but is also good served cold as a lunchbox or picnic salad.

SERVES 4 Ⓥ

WORTH THE EFFORT

Syns per serving
Green: Free
Original: 7½

Preparation time 20 minutes
Cooking time 15–20 minutes

175g/6oz bulgur wheat

500g/1lb 2oz midi vine tomatoes

Fry Light

salt and freshly ground black pepper

1 red chilli, deseeded and finely sliced

6 spring onions, thinly sliced

110g/4oz baby leaf spinach

a large handful of mint leaves

a large handful of coriander leaves

juice of 1 lemon

1. Place the bulgur wheat in a large, heatproof bowl and pour over 350ml/12fl oz of boiling water. Cover and leave to soak for 15–20 minutes until all the water is absorbed.

2. Preheat the oven to 200°C/Gas 6. Place the tomatoes on a non-stick baking sheet and spray with Fry Light. Season well and roast in the oven for 15–20 minutes. Remove and transfer to a wide, shallow salad bowl with any juices.

3. Fluff up the bulgur grains with a fork and add to the tomatoes along with the chilli, spring onions, spinach and herbs. Stir in the lemon juice, season well and toss to combine. Serve immediately.

> **Tomatoes**
> The warm, heady smell of ripe tomatoes sums up summer. Choose round English varieties for salads and sandwiches, cherry or plum tomatoes for roasting and using in pasta sauces, or beef tomatoes for slicing or stuffing. All tomatoes are high in vitamin C, and cooked tomatoes are especially rich in the powerful antioxidant lycopene. Our Roasted Tomato and Bulgur Salad is bursting with fresh summer flavours.

potato, fresh bean
and herb salad

The fresh peas and beans in this simple salad give it lots of crunch and flavour – a brilliant lunchtime dish!

SERVES 4 ⓥ

WORTH THE EFFORT

Syns per serving

Green: ½

Original: 3

Preparation time 5 minutes

Cooking time about 10 minutes

200g/7oz potatoes, peeled and cut into 1.5cm/¾in cubes

300g/11oz sugar snap peas, trimmed

300g/11oz French beans, trimmed

200g/7oz broad beans, shelled

6 tbsp finely chopped mixed herbs, such as tarragon, dill, parsley and chives

For the dressing

juice of 1 lemon

1 tsp runny honey

1 tsp Dijon mustard

8 tbsp fat-free vinaigrette or French-style salad dressing

salt and freshly ground black pepper

To garnish

lemon zest (optional)

finely chopped red chilli (optional)

1. Boil the potatoes in a large pan of lightly salted water and cook for 8–10 minutes, or until just tender. Drain well and set aside.

2. Bring a large pan of lightly salted water to the boil and add the peas and beans. Bring back to the boil, then drain and refresh under cold running water. Drain again and place in a salad bowl with the potatoes and chopped herbs.

3. Mix together all the dressing ingredients, season well and pour over the vegetables. Toss well and garnish with the lemon zest and red chilli, if using, before serving.

summer potato, celery
and herb salad

Colourful and bursting with the fragrant flavours of dill and mint, this salad will become a regular favourite way into the summer!

SERVES 4 ⓥ

EASY

Syns per serving

Green: 1

Original: 5½

Preparation time 10 minutes

500g/1lb 2oz potatoes, peeled, cooked and cut into 2cm/¾in cubes

6 spring onions, finely sliced

12 cherry tomatoes, halved

4 sticks celery, finely sliced

110g/4oz green seedless grapes, halved

6 tbsp finely chopped dill

6 tbsp finely chopped mint

For the dressing

6 tbsp Hellmann's Extra Light Mayonnaise

110g/4oz very low fat natural yogurt

1 tsp finely grated garlic

salt and freshly ground black pepper

1. Place the potatoes and spring onions in a shallow serving bowl. Add the tomatoes, celery, grapes and chopped herbs.

2. Mix together the dressing ingredients and season well. Pour over the salad and toss well. Serve at room temperature.

italian-style
warm fennel salad

Here is a great dinner party starter, but it could also be used to accompany roasted meat or fish on an Original day.

SERVES 4 ⓥ
EASY
Syns per serving
Original: Free
Green: Free

Preparation time 10 minutes
Cooking time 20–25 minutes

3 large fennel bulbs
2 large red onions, peeled
Fry Light
400ml/14fl oz water, or vegetable stock made with Vecon
salt and freshly ground black pepper
finely grated orange zest

1. Preheat the oven to 220°C/Gas 7. Trim the fennel and cut into thick slices. Place in an ovenproof dish in a single layer. Cut the onions into thick wedges and scatter over the fennel.

2. Spray Fry Light evenly over the vegetables and pour in the water or stock. Season well and cover loosely with a scrunched-up piece of foil.

3. Bake in the oven for 20–25 minutes, or until tender. Sprinkle over the orange zest and serve warm or at room temperature.

bacon-wrapped cod

Use any thick, firm white fish fillet for this recipe, but do make sure it is skinned. The saltiness of the bacon makes a great contrast.

SERVES 4

WORTH THE EFFORT

Syns per serving
Original: Free
Green: 15

Preparation time 5 minutes
Cooking time 20 minutes

salt and freshly ground black pepper

4 x 250g/9oz thick cod fillets, skinned

4 garlic cloves, peeled and finely chopped

4 tbsp finely grated lemon zest

8 tbsp finely chopped flat-leaf parsley

12 lean bacon rashers

To serve

grilled vine tomatoes

steamed green beans

1. Preheat the oven to 200°C/Gas 6. Line a non-stick baking sheet with baking parchment.

2. Season the cod fillets well on both sides. Sprinkle over the garlic, half the lemon zest and half the parsley.

3. Wrap each fillet with three bacon rashers to cover evenly, and place on the prepared baking sheet. Sprinkle over the remaining lemon zest and parsley and bake in the oven for 20 minutes, or until the fish is cooked through.

4. Serve immediately with vine tomatoes and green beans.

barbecue plaice
with red pepper salsa

The delicate, creamy texture of the plaice is complemented perfectly by the tangy pepper and tomato salsa.

SERVES 4

EASY

Syns per serving

Original: Free

Green: 9

Preparation time 10 minutes plus standing

Cooking time 5–6 minutes

4 x 250g/9oz plaice fillets

1 tbsp finely grated lemon zest

2 tbsp very finely snipped chives

Fry Light

For the salsa

1 red pepper, finely diced

1 tomato, finely diced

1 small red onion, peeled and finely diced

1 tsp yellow mustard seeds

1 tsp artificial sweetener

1 tbsp wine vinegar

salt and freshly ground black pepper

1. Make the salsa by combining all the ingredients in a bowl and season well. Cover and stand at room temperature for 30 minutes.

2. Place the fish on a grill rack and sprinkle over the lemon zest and chives. Season well and spray with Fry Light. Place on a barbecue or under a hot grill and cook for 5–6 minutes, or until the fish is cooked through. Remove from the heat and serve with the salsa.

Peppers

Red, yellow, orange and green: peppers are a delicious way to 'eat a rainbow' of vitamins and antioxidants. A staple of the healthy Mediterranean diet, they're eaten raw in salads or salsas, as in our Barbecue Plaice with Red Pepper Salsa, roasted with grilled meat and fish, or stuffed with tasty rice or meat fillings. Hot or cold, raw or cooked, they'll brighten any summer meal.

chargrilled tuna
with herby beans

Take care not to overcook the tuna because this can make it dry. Ideally, it needs to be slightly pink on the inside.

SERVES 4
EASY
Syns per serving
Original: Free
Green: 18

Preparation time 10 minutes
Cooking time about 20 minutes

Fry Light

2 red onions, peeled and finely chopped

3 garlic cloves, peeled and finely chopped

6 plum tomatoes, roughly chopped

400g/14oz green beans, trimmed and halved

salt and freshly ground black pepper

2 tbsp very finely chopped mixed herbs

4 x 250g/9oz thick tuna steaks

finely grated zest of 1 lemon

1. Spray a large, non-stick frying pan with Fry Light and add the onions, garlic, tomatoes and green beans. Bring to the boil, reduce the heat to medium-low, cover and simmer gently for 12–15 minutes, stirring occasionally. Season, stir in the chopped herbs and set aside to keep warm.

2. Lightly spray the tuna with Fry Light, sprinkle with the lemon zest and season well. Heat a non-stick ridged griddle pan over a high heat and, when very hot, cook the tuna in it for 1–2 minutes on each side, or until cooked to your liking.

3. Divide the bean mixture between 4 warmed plates, top with the tuna and serve.

spicy monkfish stew

Monkfish has a superb firm texture and a delicious sweetness, which make it ideal for serving in a hearty fish stew.

SERVES 4 ❅

WORTH THE EFFORT

Syns per serving
Original: Free
Green: 7

Preparation time 15 minutes
Cooking time 35 minutes

Fry Light

2 red peppers, deseeded and cut into fine dice

1 onion, peeled, halved and sliced

1 red chilli, finely sliced

3 garlic cloves, peeled and finely chopped

2 large tomatoes, roughly chopped

1 litre/1¾ pints chicken stock made with Bovril

1 tsp sweet smoked paprika

2 bay leaves

800g/1lb 12oz monkfish fillets, cut into big bite-sized pieces

salt and freshly ground black pepper

4 tbsp torn flat-leaf parsley

To serve

lemon wedges

1. Spray a large non-stick wok or frying pan with Fry Light. Place over a medium heat and add the peppers, onion, chilli and garlic. Stir-fry for 4–5 minutes, then add the tomatoes and stock and bring to the boil.

2. Add the paprika and bay leaves, reduce the heat to a simmer, cover and cook gently for 20 minutes.

3. Add the fish and simmer gently for 10 minutes, or until cooked through. Season well.

4. Scatter the parsley into the stew and serve in warmed soup plates with the lemon wedges for squeezing over.

red mullet
in vine leaves

Vine leaves, preserved in brine, are available in packets or jars. They must be rinsed thoroughly in cold water before use.

SERVES 4

WORTH THE EFFORT

Syns per serving
Original: Free
Green: 18

Preparation time 10 minutes
Cooking time about 8 minutes

4 x 350g/12oz red mullet, cleaned, gutted and scaled

salt and freshly ground black pepper

8 tbsp roughly chopped flat-leaf parsley

2 tbsp finely grated lemon zest

1 tbsp finely chopped garlic

2 tsp finely chopped red chilli

4 large vine leaves in brine, rinsed and patted dry

To serve

lemon wedges

1. Place the fish on a work surface and season well inside and out with salt and pepper.

2. In a bowl, mix together the parsley, lemon zest, garlic and chilli, and use this mixture to stuff each fish.

3. Wrap each fish tightly in a vine leaf, with the head and tail exposed, and place on a rack. Cook under a medium-hot grill or over a hot barbecue for 3–4 minutes on each side, or until cooked through.

4. Transfer the wrapped fish to warmed plates and serve with lemon wedges. To eat, unwrap and discard the vine leaves and squeeze lemon juice over the fish.

moroccan-style
squid

You can now buy ready-cleaned squid from fishmongers or larger supermarkets, which will save you time and effort in preparation.

SERVES 4

WORTH THE EFFORT

Syns per serving

Original: Free

Green: 10

Preparation time 20 minutes plus marinating

Cooking time 3–4 minutes

5 tbsp finely chopped coriander

5 tbsp finely chopped flat-leaf parsley

1 tbsp paprika

1 tbsp ground coriander

1 tbsp ground cumin

1 tsp cayenne pepper

4 garlic cloves, peeled and crushed

50g/2oz very low fat natural yogurt

juice of 1 lemon

salt and freshly ground black pepper

8 medium squid (approx. 150g/5oz each), slit down one side of each tube

Fry Light

1. Place the chopped herbs in a mini food processor with the spices, garlic, yogurt and lemon juice. Season well and blend to make a smooth paste. Transfer to a bowl and set aside.

2. Open out each piece of squid, spread flat and make diagonal cuts on the top side only. Add to the paste mixture in the bowl and stir to coat well. Cover and allow to marinate in the fridge overnight.

3. Half an hour before cooking, place 16 wooden skewers to soak in warm water. Take a piece of squid and insert a soaked skewer along one cut edge, pushing it in and out as though inserting a safety pin. Insert another skewer along the other cut edge. This keeps the squid flat. Repeat with the remaining skewers and squid pieces.

4. Spray the squid with Fry Light and cook under a preheated grill or on a barbecue for 3–4 minutes, turning once. Remove and serve immediately

> **Squid**
> Also known as calamari, squid is popular in Greek and Spanish cooking, as well as in our more unusual Moroccan-style Squid. Baby squid can be cooked whole, while large squid are often stuffed, or cut into rings and quickly stir-fried over a high heat with garlic, parsley and chilli. Squid is a healthy choice too, as it contains various B vitamins and minerals.

grilled chicken pinchitos

Pinchitos are Spanish-style chicken skewers, which are served as a tapas dish or a main meal. They are also perfect barbecue fare.

SERVES 4 ❄
EASY
Syns per serving
Original: Free
Green: 10½

Preparation time 10 minutes plus marinating
Cooking time 10 minutes

2 tsp ground cumin

1 tsp ground coriander

1 tsp sweet smoked paprika

2 tsp dried thyme

salt

800g/1lb 12oz chicken breasts, skinless and boneless, cut into small cubes

1 dried bay leaf, crumbled

3 garlic cloves, peeled and crushed

juice of 1 lemon

Fry Light

3–4 small red onions, peeled and cut into wedges

To serve
tomato and cucumber salad

1. Combine all the spices in a bowl, mix in the thyme and season with salt. Rub this mixture into the chicken and place in a dish with the bay leaf and garlic evenly distributed. Stir in the lemon juice and spray with Fry Light. Cover and marinate in the fridge overnight.

2. When ready to cook, thread the chicken onto 8 skewers, alternating each piece with an onion wedge. Cook under a hot grill or over a barbecue for 4–5 minutes on each side, or until cooked through. Serve immediately with a tomato and cucumber salad.

grilled chicken salad

Garlic, ginger, saffron and cinnamon mixed with yogurt make a tasty marinade for succulent chicken thighs. Use chicken breast if you prefer for this simple, tasty salad.

SERVES 4

EASY

Syns per serving
Original: 1
Green: 11½

Preparation time 10 minutes plus marinating

Cooking time 10–12 minutes

800g/1lb 12oz chicken thighs, skinless and boneless, cut into bite-sized pieces

110g/4oz very low fat natural yogurt

2 tsp finely grated ginger

4 garlic cloves, peeled and crushed

2 large pinches of saffron threads

1 tsp ground cinnamon

1 tsp chilli powder

salt and freshly ground black pepper

200g/7oz wild rocket

2 ripe tomatoes, roughly chopped

1 red onion, peeled, halved and thinly sliced

For the dressing

6 tbsp Hellmann's Extra Light Mayonnaise

110g/4oz very low fat natural fromage frais

finely grated zest of 1 lemon

1. Place the chicken in a large mixing bowl. Mix together the yogurt, ginger, garlic, saffron, cinnamon and chilli powder. Season well and pour over the chicken. Toss well, cover and marinate in the fridge for 6–8 hours, or overnight if time permits.

2. Thread the chicken pieces onto 8 metal skewers. Cook over a barbecue or under a medium-hot grill for 10–12 minutes, turning once, until the chicken is cooked through.

3. Remove the chicken from the skewers and place in a large salad bowl with the rocket, tomatoes and onion.

4. Mix together all the dressing ingredients. Season well, drizzle over the salad and serve.

chicken, pork and bacon burgers

Brilliant barbecue food or an anytime snack. These burgers can be served in wholemeal rolls if you like (6 Syns per 50g/2oz).

SERVES 4 ❄

EASY

Syns per serving
Original: Free
Green: 17½

Preparation time 15 minutes
Cooking time about 12 minutes

500g/1lb 2oz extra-lean minced pork

500g/1lb 2oz lean minced chicken

4 tbsp very finely chopped shallots

2 tsp Worcestershire sauce

2 garlic cloves, peeled and crushed

4 tbsp finely chopped flat-leaf parsley

salt and freshly ground black pepper

Fry Light

8 lean bacon rashers, grilled

To serve
crisp green lettuce
sliced tomatoes
sliced onion
sliced cucumber

1. Place the pork and chicken in a bowl, add the shallots, Worcestershire sauce, garlic and parsley and combine thoroughly, using your fingers. Season well, mix again and divide into 8 portions. Shape each portion into a flat 'burger'.

2. Spray the burgers with Fry Light and cook under a hot grill for 5–6 minutes on each side, or until cooked to your liking. Remove and keep warm.

3. Place 2 burgers on each warmed plate and top each serving with 2 grilled bacon rashers. Serve with a crisp mixed salad on the side.

grilled pork steaks
with plum and mango salsa

Always try to use the ripest mangoes you can find as they will make a considerable difference to the taste of the salsa.

SERVES 4

EASY

Syns per serving
Original: Free
Green: 7½

Preparation time 10 minutes
Cooking time under 15 minutes

4 x 150g/5oz lean pork loin steaks

Fry Light

salt and freshly ground black pepper

For the salsa

8 ripe plums, stoned and cut into small dice

2 ripe mangoes, peeled, stoned and cut into 1cm/½in dice

1 red pepper, deseeded and cut into 1cm/½in dice

juice of 1 lime

a small handful of chopped mint and parsley

1. Lightly spray the pork with Fry Light and season well. Place under a medium-hot grill or on a hot griddle pan and cook for 5–6 minutes on each side, or until cooked through.

2. While the pork is cooking, combine all the salsa ingredients in a bowl, season well and set aside.

3. When ready to eat, place the pork on warmed plates and serve with the salsa.

> **Pork**
> Often associated with winter roasts, pork is also perfect for summer cooking. Cuts such as escalopes, loin steaks or medallions are ideal for grilling, especially with a tangy marinade, or when served with a zingy accompaniment, as in our Grilled Pork Steaks with Plum and Mango Salsa. Lean pork is a good source of vitamin B_6 and zinc as well as protein – a great low-fat way to fill up.

spanish-style
meatballs

Moorish in origin, these golden-brown, spiced meatballs are tossed in a flavoured tomato sauce and are a tapas favourite.

SERVES 4 ✳

WORTH THE EFFORT

Syns per serving

Original: Free

Green: 4

Preparation time 15 minutes plus chilling

Cooking time about 1 hour

300g/11oz extra-lean minced pork

3 garlic cloves, peeled and crushed

1 tsp ground cumin

1 tsp ground coriander

1 tsp ground nutmeg

1 tsp ground cinnamon

salt and freshly ground black pepper

For the sauce

Fry Light

1 small onion, peeled and finely chopped

1 garlic clove, peeled and crushed

1 x 400g can chopped tomatoes

1 tsp artificial sweetener

1 tsp sweet pimenton or mild paprika

1. Place the mince, garlic and spices in a bowl and mix with your hands until well combined. Season well and mix again. Cover and chill in the fridge for 1 hour to allow the flavours to develop.

2. Meanwhile, make the sauce. Spray a large frying pan with Fry Light and put over a high heat. When hot, add the onion and garlic and cook, stirring, over a medium heat for 5–6 minutes.

3. Stir in the tomatoes, sweetener and pimenton and bring to the boil. Reduce the heat, cover and simmer gently for 25–30 minutes, stirring occasionally. Season well.

4. When the meat has chilled, roll it into walnut-sized balls. Spray a non-stick frying pan with Fry Light, add half the meatballs and stir-fry over a medium heat for 2–3 minutes, until browned. Drain on kitchen paper and repeat with the remaining balls.

5. Place the sauce mixture over a medium heat and add the cooked meatballs. Stir and simmer gently for 8–10 minutes. Serve hot.

summer french-style herb cake

This savoury cake is great eaten hot, but equally good served cold, so it's perfect for picnics and lunchboxes.

SERVES 4 Ⓥ ❋
EASY
Syns per serving
Original: Free
Green: Free

Preparation time 10 minutes
Cooking time 15 minutes

Fry Light

8 eggs, lightly beaten

10 tbsp finely chopped mixed fresh herbs, such as tarragon, chives, parsley, mint and thyme

salt and freshly ground black pepper

2 tomatoes, finely diced

a pinch of grated nutmeg

To serve

tomato and red onion salad

1. Spray a large, non-stick frying pan with Fry Light and place over a medium heat. Mix together the eggs and the herbs and season well. Pour into the pan and swirl to cover the base.

2. Evenly scatter the tomatoes and nutmeg into the pan and cook gently for 8–10 minutes, or until the bottom of the egg mixture is set and golden.

3. Place the pan under a hot grill and cook for 2–3 minutes, or until the top of the 'cake' is just set. Serve immediately with a tomato and red onion salad.

broad bean and lemon risotto

Broad beans should be bought and used as fresh as possible, otherwise the skins tend to be tough. If in doubt, peel them before use.

SERVES 4 ✤

WORTH THE EFFORT

Syns per serving
With Parmesan
Green: 1
Original: 15

Without Parmesan
Green: Free
Original: 14

Preparation time 15 minutes
Cooking time about 45 minutes

Fry Light

1 small onion, peeled and finely chopped

2 garlic cloves, peeled and finely chopped

250g/9oz Arborio or risotto rice

2 tsp dried mixed herbs

900ml/1½ pints boiling hot chicken stock made with Bovril

300g/11oz broad beans, shelled

finely grated zest of 1 lemon

salt and freshly ground black pepper

6 tbsp finely chopped dill

To serve

2 tbsp grated Parmesan cheese (optional)

1. Spray a large frying pan with Fry Light and place over a medium heat. Add the onion, garlic and rice and stir-fry for 5–6 minutes. Add the dried herbs and a ladleful of the stock, stirring until absorbed before adding another ladleful. Continue adding a ladleful at a time, stirring constantly, until all the stock has been used up.

2. Stir in the broad beans and lemon zest and continue cooking and stirring gently for about 20–25 minutes. The rice should be creamy and al dente (cooked through but retaining a slight bite).

3. Remove from the heat, season well and stir in the dill. Serve immediately in warmed bowls, sprinkled with grated Parmesan, if using.

Broad beans

Tender, young broad beans are a delicious match for fresh summer tastes such as mint, lemon, garlic and parsley, as in our Broad Bean and Lemon Risotto. They're a good source of vegetable protein and also soluble fibre, which can help to regulate blood cholesterol. Lightly cooked broad beans are a tasty addition to salads, especially with cheese or bacon.

fennel and shallot rice

The Hindi word *basmati* means 'fragrant one', and the rice of this name is considered to be the prince of its relatives. It's used here to create a simple yet tasty lunchtime dish that's ready in no time at all.

SERVES 4 Ⓥ ❅
EASY
Syns per serving
Green: Free
Original: 12½

Preparation time 20 minutes
Cooking time about 20 minutes

275g/10oz dried basmati rice
Fry Light
4 shallots, peeled and finely chopped
2 tsp fennel seeds
2 garlic cloves, peeled and finely chopped
4 ripe tomatoes, skinned, deseeded and finely chopped
salt and freshly ground black pepper
2 tbsp finely chopped coriander leaves

1. Wash the rice in several changes of cold water, then leave to soak in a bowl of cold water for 20 minutes. Drain thoroughly and set aside.

2. Spray a heavy-based saucepan with Fry Light and place over a medium heat. Add the shallots, fennel seeds and garlic and fry for 4–5 minutes.

3. Add the tomatoes and the rice and stir-fry for 2–3 minutes. Season well, then pour in 500ml/18fl oz of hot water. Bring to the boil, cover tightly and reduce the heat to low. Cook for 8–10 minutes, then remove from the heat (keeping the lid on) and allow to stand for 10 minutes.

4. When ready to serve, fluff up the rice grains with a fork. Stir in the coriander and serve immediately.

tip

To skin tomatoes, use a sharp knife to cut a small cross in the base of each one and put them in a bowl of boiling water for a minute: the skins will then peel off easily. If you are in a rush, use a can of chopped tomatoes, but drain off the juice before using.

asparagus
with minted couscous

Asparagus is available almost all year round, but outside the season (late spring to early summer) it will have been imported and will not have the wonderful flavour of home-produced varieties.

SERVES 4 Ⓥ
EASY
Syns per serving
Green: Free
Original: 5

Preparation time 10–12 minutes
Cooking time 5 minutes

110g/4oz couscous
salt and freshly ground black pepper
500g/1lb 2oz asparagus tips
2 courgettes, cut into 1cm/½in cubes
a small handful of mint leaves, roughly torn
6 tbsp fat-free French-style salad dressing

1. Place the couscous in a wide, heatproof bowl, season well and pour over just enough boiling water to cover. Put a plate or cling film over the bowl and allow to stand for 10–12 minutes, or until all the water has been absorbed.

2. Meanwhile, place the asparagus in a large saucepan of lightly salted boiling water and cook for 4–5 minutes, adding the courgettes for the last minute. Drain thoroughly.

3. Fluff up the couscous grains with a fork and add the asparagus, courgettes, mint and dressing. Toss well and serve immediately.

> **Asparagus**
> Look out for English asparagus from late May: its elegant, purply-green spears taste wonderful and are a good source of folate and vitamins A, C and E. Enjoy asparagus lightly boiled or steamed, with a twist of black pepper or fat-free vinaigrette; dip the spears into a soft-boiled egg; or for a summery main course, try our Asparagus with Minted Couscous (above), or Asparagus, Ginger and Noodle Stir-Fry (page 84).

asparagus, ginger
and noodle stir-fry

A crunchy, filling stir-fry that will have the family coming back for more; it's a good thing it takes only minutes to prepare!

SERVES 4 Ⓥ

WORTH THE EFFORT

Syns per serving

Green: Free

Original: 11½

Preparation time 5 minutes

Cooking time 10 minutes

400g/14oz asparagus tips

250g/9oz dried medium egg noodles

Fry Light

10 spring onions, cut into 4cm/1½in lengths

2 garlic cloves, peeled and crushed

1 tsp finely grated ginger

200g/7oz baby whole sweetcorn

1 red pepper, finely sliced

4 tbsp dark soy sauce

1. Blanch the asparagus in a large pan of lightly salted boiling water for 2–3 minutes. Drain and set aside.

2. Meanwhile, cook the noodles according to the packet instructions. Spray a large, non-stick wok with Fry Light and place over a high heat.

3. Add the asparagus, spring onions, garlic, ginger, sweetcorn and red pepper and stir-fry over a high heat for 6–8 minutes.

4. Drain the cooked noodles and add to the wok with the soy sauce. Toss well and stir-fry for 1–2 minutes. Transfer to warmed bowls and serve hot.

tagliatelle
with summer vegetables

You can use any seasonal vegetables you like in this recipe, giving you endless variations of taste and texture.

SERVES 4 Ⓥ

EASY

Syns per serving
Green: Free
Original: 15

Preparation time 15 minutes
Cooking time 10 minutes

300g/11oz dried tagliatelle
Fry Light
2 garlic cloves, peeled and crushed
150g/5oz baby leeks, thinly sliced
6 baby courgettes, thinly sliced
125g/4½oz fine asparagus tips
110g/4oz fresh or frozen peas
salt and freshly ground black pepper
juice and finely grated zest of 1 lemon
8 tbsp finely chopped mixed herbs

1. Cook the pasta according to the packet instructions, then drain and set aside.

2. While the pasta is cooking, spray a large non-stick frying pan with Fry Light and place over a medium heat. Add the garlic, leeks, courgettes, asparagus and peas and stir-fry for 5–6 minutes.

3. Season well, then add the pasta, lemon juice and zest. Toss well and cook for 2–3 minutes, or until piping hot. Check the seasoning, then stir in the chopped herbs and serve immediately in warmed pasta bowls.

creamy
courgette linguine with mint

You could use baby courgettes in this recipe if you wish (you will need 8–10 of them); just slice them very thinly and follow the recipe.

SERVES 4 Ⓥ
EASY

Syns per serving

With Parmesan

Green: 1

Original: 16

Without Parmesan

Green: Free

Original: 15

Preparation time 15 minutes

Cooking time 20 minutes

350g/12oz dried linguine or spaghetti

Fry Light

2 garlic cloves, peeled and crushed

1 red chilli, deseeded and finely chopped

2 large courgettes, coarsely grated

150g/5oz Quark soft cheese

salt and freshly ground black pepper

6 tbsp finely chopped fresh mint leaves

To serve

2 tbsp grated Parmesan cheese (optional)

1. Cook the pasta according to the packet instructions. Drain and set aside.

2. Meanwhile, spray a large, non-stick frying pan with Fry Light and place over a medium heat. Add the garlic, chilli and courgettes and cook, stirring occasionally, for 8–10 minutes, or until the courgettes have softened.

3. Stir in the Quark and continue to stir and cook for 5–6 minutes. Season well and add the drained pasta and chopped mint. Toss well and remove from the heat.

4. Serve in warmed pasta plates and sprinkle with Parmesan cheese, if using.

mangetout
with tarragon

The only difficulty you'll have with this recipe is deciding what to serve it with – the choice is all yours!

SERVES 4 Ⓥ ❋

EASY

Syns per serving
Original: Free
Green: Free

Preparation time 10 minutes
Cooking time 15 minutes

800g/1lb 2oz mangetout, trimmed

Fry Light

1 garlic clove, peeled and finely chopped

6 shallots, peeled, halved and thinly sliced

salt and freshly ground black pepper

4 tbsp very finely chopped tarragon

1. Blanch the mangetout in a large saucepan of lightly salted boiling water for 2–3 minutes. Drain thoroughly and set aside.

2. Spray a large, non-stick wok or frying pan with Fry Light and place over a medium heat. Add the garlic and shallots and stir-fry for 3–4 minutes. Turn the heat to high and add the mangetout. Season well and stir-fry for 3–4 minutes, or until tender.

3. Remove from the heat and stir in the chopped tarragon just before serving.

crushed potatoes
with chives

Waxy potatoes work best in this recipe, and commonly available varieties include Charlotte, Maris Bard and Maris Peer.

SERVES 4 Ⓥ ❄

WORTH THE EFFORT

Syns per serving
Green: Free
Original: 7

Preparation time 10 minutes
Cooking time about 30 minutes

800g/1lb 12oz small, waxy new potatoes (each weighing about 40g/1½oz)
Fry Light
10 shallots, peeled
6–8 garlic cloves, unpeeled
4–5 fresh bay leaves
1 tbsp pink peppercorns
sea salt and freshly ground black pepper
250ml/9fl oz water, or vegetable stock made with Vecon
8 tbsp finely snipped chives

1. Bring a large pan of lightly salted water to the boil. Add the potatoes and cook for 4–5 minutes. Drain thoroughly and then place on a clean work surface. Using a wooden mallet or a large pestle, hold each potato and bash it lightly enough to crack open, but not hard enough to smash.

2. Spray the base of a wide, heavy-based pan with Fry Light and arrange the potatoes and shallots in it. Tuck the garlic cloves and bay leaves among them and sprinkle with the peppercorns. Season well and spray again with Fry Light.

3. Pour in the water or stock, cover with a tight-fitting lid and cook on a medium-low heat for about 20 minutes, or until the potatoes are tender. (You might need to add a little more water or stock towards the end, but the liquid should be well reduced by the time the contents are done.)

4. Remove the pan from the heat, stir in the chives and serve immediately.

savoury
summer vegetable loaf

You could use any of your favourite vegetables in this recipe in place of those suggested, making this dish a year-round treat!

SERVES 4 Ⓥ ❄
EASY

Syns per serving
Green: Free
Original: 5½

Preparation time 5–10 minutes
Cooking time 40–45 minutes ⟍

or 25 min. in Halogen oven.

Fry Light

400g/14oz sweetcorn kernels

200g/7oz canned or bottled red peppers, drained and cut into small dice

200g/7oz green beans, blanched and cut into 1cm/½in lengths

4 large eggs, lightly beaten

2 tbsp finely chopped fresh mixed herbs of your choice

salt and freshly ground black pepper

To serve

crisp green salad

1. Spray a small, non-stick loaf tin with Fry Light and line the base with non-stick baking parchment. Preheat the oven to 200°C/Gas 6.

2. Place the sweetcorn, peppers, beans, eggs and herbs in a bowl. Season well and mix thoroughly. Pour this mixture into the prepared tin and bake in the oven for 40–45 minutes, or until the mixture is just set.

3. Remove from the oven and allow to rest for 10 minutes before turning out onto a board. Cut into thick slices and serve immediately with a crisp green salad.

grilled sweetcorn cobettes
with lime, chilli and herb 'butter'

Perfect finger food for a barbecue, or great as a lunchtime snack. You could use whole cobs, if you prefer.

SERVES 4 ⓥ

WORTH THE EFFORT

Syns per serving

Green: 1½

Original: 18

Preparation time 5 minutes

Cooking time about 4–5 minutes

4 x 300g/11oz sweetcorn cobs

For the 'butter'

3 tbsp very low fat spread, softened

finely grated zest of 1 lime

1 tbsp finely chopped red chilli

1 tbsp very finely chopped parsley

1. Cut each corn cob into 3 equal pieces or cobettes. Insert a wooden or metal skewer through the middle of each cobette and place on a barbecue or hot griddle pan. Cook, turning frequently, for 4–5 minutes, or until lightly charred and blistered in places.

2. Meanwhile, mix together all the 'butter' ingredients and set aside. When the cobettes are cooked, remove from the heat and serve immediately with the butter brushed all over.

Sweetcorn

Golden cobs of corn are a sure sign that summer has arrived. While they're rich in carotene, and also a good source of vitamin C, potassium, magnesium and phosphorus, why not enjoy them simply for their delightful sweetness? This is best when the cobs are really fresh and cooked simply, as in our recipe for Grilled Sweetcorn Cobettes above.

french beans
with black mustard seeds

A great accompaniment to meat or fish on an Original day, this would go equally well with rice or pasta on a Green day.

SERVES 4 ⓥ ❅
EASY
Syns per serving
Original: 5½
Green: 5½

Preparation time 15 minutes
Cooking time about 1 hour

Fry Light
2 tsp black mustard seeds
1 onion, peeled and finely chopped
2 garlic cloves, peeled and crushed
1 x 400g can chopped tomatoes
2 bay leaves
2 tbsp finely chopped parsley
4 tbsp finely chopped dill
salt and freshly ground black pepper
1 tsp hot paprika
½ tsp artificial sweetener
800g/1lb 12oz French beans, trimmed
175g/6oz feta cheese

1. Spray a large frying pan with Fry Light and place over a medium heat. Add the black mustard seeds and onion and stir-fry for 5–6 minutes, or until soft.

2. Add the garlic, tomatoes and 450ml/16fl oz of water. Stir in the bay leaves, parsley and half the dill. Season well, stir in the paprika and sweetener and bring to the boil.

3. Partially cover, lower the heat and simmer gently for 25–30 minutes, until the sauce has thickened. Add the beans and simmer gently for another 10–12 minutes.

4. Cut the feta into chunky cubes, add to the pan and cook gently for 3–4 minutes. Remove from the heat and serve in warmed bowls, scattered with the remaining dill.

custard
and mixed berry pavlova

This dessert is heaven on a plate – both to look at and to eat! You can make it even more special by drizzling melted dark chocolate over the top (1½ Syns per 1 level tsp) just before serving.

SERVES 6 Ⓥ
EXTRA EASY
Syns per serving
Original: 5½
Green: 5½

Preparation time 10 minutes

110g/4oz raspberries
110g/4oz small strawberries
110g/4oz blueberries
110g/4oz blackberries
artificial sweetener, to taste
1 meringue pavlova
8 tbsp canned low fat custard

To serve
1 tsp icing sugar

1. Mix the berries together in a bowl with the sweetener and lightly crush a few of them with the back of a fork to release some of the juices.

2. Place the meringue on a serving plate and fill with the custard. Top the custard with the berries and serve dusted with a little icing sugar.

> **Summer berries**
> Whether you pick wild berries or buy cultivated ones, these delicate soft fruits have wonderful flavour and are always a treat. We've used a combination of fresh berries in our Custard and Mixed Berry Pavlova: succulent strawberries, intensely flavoured raspberries, juicy blackberries and sweet blueberries.

vanilla and gooseberry fools

This traditional summer pudding is made using a peculiarly British favourite of the fruit world. It's easy to prepare, and low in Syns too!

SERVES 4 ⓥ

WORTH THE EFFORT

Syns per serving
Original: 1
Green: 1

Preparation time 10 minutes plus chilling
Cooking time 10–12 minutes

400g/14oz gooseberries

2–3 tbsp artificial sweetener

600g/1lb 6oz very low fat vanilla yogurt

1 small egg white

To serve

4 tbsp very low fat natural fromage frais

1. Top and tail the gooseberries and place them in a saucepan with 150ml/5fl oz of water and the sweetener. Bring to the boil, then simmer gently for 10–12 minutes, or until soft and pulpy. Remove from the heat and allow to cool completely. Chill in the fridge for 2–3 hours.

2. Place the yogurt in a large mixing bowl and gently stir in the gooseberry mixture until you have a marbled effect.

3. Whisk the egg white in a separate bowl until softly peaked, then fold into the gooseberry mixture with a metal spoon.

4. Spoon this mixture into 4 chilled dessert bowls or glasses and chill for 2–3 hours, before serving topped with a spoonful of fromage frais.

Gooseberries

Yellow or red gooseberries can be eaten raw, but green gooseberries are best stewed with sweetener and served in desserts such as meringues, ice cream or our creamy Vanilla and Gooseberry Fools. High in vitamin C and soluble fibre, sweet-sour gooseberries are also a classic accompaniment to oily fish and rich meat, such as mackerel, duck or goose.

minted three-melon
salad with cherries

The sweetness of the cherries and the refreshing taste of the melons make this a mouth-watering and colourful way to finish off any meal.

SERVES 4 Ⓥ
EXTRA EASY
Syns per serving
Original: Free
Green: Free

Preparation time 10 minutes
plus chilling

½ a watermelon
½ a honeydew melon
½ a Galia or cantaloupe melon
200g/7oz cherries, pitted
24 mint leaves
1–2 tbsp artificial sweetener

To garnish
sprigs of mint

1. Discard the seeds of the melons and scoop out the flesh with a melon baller. Alternatively, cut into wedges, remove the rind and cut the flesh into 2cm/¾in cubes. Mix the melons and cherries together in a shallow serving bowl.

2. Place the mint on a board and sprinkle over the sweetener. Using a sharp knife, chop the mint finely. Sprinkle this mixture over the fruit and toss gently to coat evenly. Chill for 1 hour before serving, garnished with the mint sprigs.

Melon
Especially refreshing during the summer, melons need little more than chilling and sprinkling with ground ginger, black pepper or lime to bring out their sweet, fragrant flavour. Ring the changes with orange cantaloupes (which have the most vitamin C), green Galia, yellow honeydew or bright red watermelon – or mix them together, as in our colourful Minted Three-melon Salad with Cherries.

autumn

WHAT'S IN SEASON
apples ~ aubergines ~ blackberries
butternut squash ~ cabbage ~ cauliflower ~
duck ~ mushrooms ~ mussels ~ pumpkin

creamy mushroom pâté

You could serve this pâté with vegetable crudités, such as sticks of carrot, celery and cucumber, or with wholemeal toast (6 Syns per 50g/2oz).

SERVES 4 ⓥ ❄

WORTH THE EFFORT

Syns per serving
Original: Free
Green: Free

Preparation time 20 minutes plus chilling

Cooking time 15 minutes

250g/9oz mixed mushrooms, roughly chopped

Fry Light

2 shallots, peeled and finely chopped

2 garlic cloves, peeled and finely chopped

1 tbsp finely chopped thyme leaves

salt and freshly ground black pepper

150g/5oz Quark soft cheese

1. Blend the mushrooms in a food processor.

2. Spray a large, non-stick frying pan with Fry Light and place over a high heat. Add the shallots and garlic and stir-fry for 4–5 minutes. Tip in the mushroom mixture, add the thyme and continue to stir-fry over a high heat for 8–10 minutes. Season well, then remove from the heat and allow to cool.

3. Place the Quark in a food processor with the cooled mushroom mixture. Blend until fairly smooth, then transfer to 4 individual ramekins. Cover and chill for 3–4 hours. Serve the pâté with vegetable crudités or wholemeal toast.

Mushrooms

Low in calories but high in filling power, mushrooms add bulk and flavour to pasta sauces, pie fillings and stews, and are also delicious in our Creamy Mushroom Pâté, in rich, savoury soups, or with herbs, as in our Sage and Mushroom Tortilla (page 115). Choose field, button or chestnut mushrooms for everyday cooking, or mix them with exotic varieties, such as chanterelles, morels or oysters for even deeper, richer flavours.

sweet potato wedges
with creamy herb dip

Great as a Green day snack, or to accompany griddled chicken breast or grilled fish fillet on an Original day.

SERVES 4 Ⓥ

EASY

Syns per serving
Green: Free
Original: 5½

Preparation time 15 minutes
Cooking time 25–30 minutes

600g/1lb 6oz sweet potatoes, scrubbed and dried

Fry Light

4 tsp dried chilli flakes

4–5 tsp sea salt

2 tsp dried oregano

For the dip

110g/4oz very low fat natural yogurt

50g/2oz Quark soft cheese

1 tsp finely crushed garlic

6 tbsp finely chopped mixed herbs, such as basil and parsley

salt and freshly ground black pepper

1. Preheat the oven to 180°C/Gas 4. Cut the sweet potatoes into long, thick wedges and place on a non-stick baking sheet. Lightly spray the wedges with Fry Light.

2. Mix together the chilli flakes, sea salt and oregano and toss with the sweet potatoes to coat evenly. Place in the oven and cook for 25–30 minutes, or until golden and tender.

3. Meanwhile, put all the dip ingredients into a small bowl and mix until smooth. Season and chill until needed.

4. Serve the wedges warm with the creamy herb dip.

souffléd
jacket potatoes

Maris Piper or Desirée potatoes work best in this simple lunch dish, which needs only a crisp green salad to accompany it.

SERVES 4 Ⓥ

WORTH THE EFFORT

Syns per serving

Green: 4

Original: 10

Preparation time 30 minutes

Cooking time 15–20 minutes

4 x 225g/8oz baking potatoes, scrubbed

2 eggs, separated

4 tbsp finely chopped chives

2 spring onions, finely sliced

110g/4oz grated reduced fat Cheddar cheese

salt and freshly ground black pepper

To serve

finely snipped chives

baby salad leaves

1. Boil the potatoes in a large pan of lightly salted water until tender. Drain, then cut a shallow slice from the top of each cooked potato; discard these slices. Using a teaspoon, carefully scoop out about two-thirds of the flesh and place in a large mixing bowl. Mash until smooth.

2. When the mash is cool stir in the egg yolks, chives, spring onions and cheese. Season well.

3. Preheat the oven to 200°C/Gas 6. Using an electric mixer, beat the egg whites in a small bowl until softly peaked. Fold into the potato mixture. Carefully spoon this mixture back into the hollowed-out potatoes. Place on a non-stick baking sheet and bake in the oven for 15–20 minutes, or until slightly risen and golden.

4. Serve immediately garnished with snipped chives and accompanied with baby salad leaves.

grilled garlic and herb
mussels

Mussels are really versatile and can be cooked in many ways. Here they are topped with Quark flavoured with garlic and herbs and simply grilled.

SERVES 4

WORTH THE EFFORT

Syns per serving
Original: Free
Green: 3½

Preparation time 30 minutes
Cooking time 5 minutes

24 large mussels

3 tbsp Quark soft cheese

4 tsp finely grated garlic

3 tbsp very finely chopped mixed herbs

1 red chilli, deseeded and very finely chopped

1 tsp very finely grated lime zest

salt and freshly ground black pepper

Fry Light

To serve
lime wedges

1. Wash the mussels in cold water and pull off any beards or barnacles. Discard any mussels that are open and will not close when lightly tapped. Cook the mussels in a large saucepan of boiling water for 2–3 minutes until they open. Drain thoroughly and discard any unopened mussels.

2. Arrange the mussels in their half shells on a gratin dish in a single layer.

3. Mix together the Quark, garlic, herbs, chilli and lime zest until well combined. Season and then spoon a little of the mixture over each mussel.

4. Spray the mussels with Fry Light, then place under a hot grill and cook for 1–2 minutes, or until bubbling. Serve immediately with wedges of lime to squeeze over.

Mussels

Sweet, juicy packages of healthy goodness, mussels are rich in iron, iodine and selenium, as well as vitamin B_{12}. The classic way to enjoy these shellfish is with fragrant herbs and pan juices, but they're also delicious in pasta dishes, stews and risottos – or, for an unusual twist, try our Grilled Garlic and Herb Mussels.

mint, basil and chilli-seared
scallops

King scallops have firm white flesh and, at the right time of year, orange or pale red corals. They're wonderful when cooked simply, as in this recipe.

SERVES 4

EASY

Syns per serving
Original: Free
Green: 15

Preparation time 20 minutes
plus marinating
Cooking time 5 minutes

20 king scallops, cleaned

finely grated zest and juice
of 1 lemon

2 tbsp finely chopped mixed
herbs, such as mint and basil

1 red chilli, deseeded and
finely chopped

salt and freshly ground black
pepper

Fry Light

500g/1lb 2oz pak choi,
roughly sliced

1. Place the scallops in a shallow glass or ceramic bowl in a single layer. Mix together the lemon zest and juice, chopped herbs and chilli. Season well, pour over the scallops, then cover and set aside to marinate.

2. Spray a large, non-stick frying pan with Fry Light and place over a high heat. When hot, drain the scallops (reserving the marinade) and add to the pan. Cook for 1 minute on each side, or until cooked to your liking. Pour over the reserved juices, transfer to a platter and keep warm.

3. Wipe out the pan, spray with Fry Light and place over a high heat. Add the pak choi and stir-fry over a high heat for 2–3 minutes. Divide between 4 warmed plates. Top with the scallops and their juices and serve immediately.

curried duck
with aubergine

An unusual combination of ingredients makes this simple warming dish a great suppertime treat on colder autumn days.

SERVES 4

WORTH THE EFFORT

Syns per serving

Original: Free

Green: 11

Preparation time 10 minutes

Cooking time about 25 minutes

Fry Light

2 tbsp mild or medium curry powder

600g/1lb 6oz duck breasts, skinless and sliced into thin strips

400ml/14fl oz chicken stock made with Bovril

200g/7oz canned chopped tomatoes

1 aubergine, cut into bite-sized pieces

a small handful of basil leaves

1. Spray a large, non-stick wok with Fry Light and place over a high heat. Add the curry powder and duck, and stir-fry for 1–2 minutes until sealed. Pour in the stock and tomatoes and bring to the boil.

2. Add the aubergine to the pan and cook for 15–20 minutes, or until the aubergine and duck are tender.

3. Stir in half the basil leaves and remove from the heat. Ladle the curry into deep plates or bowls, garnish with the remaining basil and serve immediately.

roast soy duck
with steamed greens

Cook the duck breasts with the skin on as it will prevent the meat from drying out, but be sure to remove it before eating.

SERVES 4

WORTH THE EFFORT

Syns per serving

Original: 1½

Green: 7½

Preparation time 10 minutes plus marinating

Cooking time 15–20 minutes

4 x 300g/11oz duck breasts

8 tbsp dark soy sauce

2 tsp ground ginger

4 tsp runny honey

1 tsp sesame oil

2 tsp Chinese five-spice powder

Fry Light

90ml/3fl oz water, or chicken stock made with Bovril

400g/14oz pak choi or Asian greens

1. Place the duck breasts on a clean work surface and make several cuts in each breast. Place in a single layer in a shallow glass or ceramic dish. Mix together the soy sauce, ginger, honey, sesame oil and five-spice powder and pour this mixture over the duck to coat well. Cover and leave to marinate for 1–2 hours.

2. Preheat the oven to 200°C/Gas 6. Transfer the duck to a non-stick baking sheet, reserving the marinade. Spray the duck with Fry Light and place in the oven for 15–20 minutes, or until cooked to your liking.

3. While the duck is cooking, place the reserved marinade in a small saucepan with the water or stock and bring to the boil. Remove from the heat and keep warm.

4. Place the greens in a steamer basket and steam for 5–6 minutes, or until just tender. Set aside and keep warm.

5. To serve, divide the steamed greens between 4 warmed plates and top with the duck. Spoon over the warm marinade and serve immediately.

> **Duck**
>
> Having a richer, deeper taste than chicken, duck is a perfect partner for punchy Chinese or Thai-style flavours, as in our Roasted Soy Duck with Steamed Greens. Barbary duck is leaner than other varieties, and ideal for dry-frying and serving with a classic orange, cherry or bramble sauce; or try it simply roasted with juicy root vegetables.

curly kale
with crispy bacon

Curly kale should be readily available, but if you can't find it, use Savoy cabbage instead; just blanch for one minute before draining.

SERVES 4 ❋

EASY

Syns per serving
Original: Free
Green: 6

Preparation time 10 minutes
Cooking time 10–12 minutes

12 lean bacon rashers

1kg/2lb 4oz curly kale, coarsely shredded

Fry Light

2 tsp caraway seeds

salt and freshly ground black pepper

1. Place the bacon on a rack and grill under a medium-high heat for 3–4 minutes, or until crisp and lightly browned. Roughly chop, then set aside and keep warm.

2. Meanwhile, blanch the kale in a large saucepan of lightly salted boiling water for 20–30 seconds. Drain and immediately plunge into cold water to stop further cooking. Drain again and place on kitchen paper to dry.

3. Spray a large, non-stick wok or frying pan with Fry Light and place over a high heat. Add the caraway seeds and bacon and stir-fry for 30 seconds. Add the kale and stir-fry for 4–5 minutes. Season well and serve immediately.

sage and mushroom tortilla

This tortilla is Free on Green and Original days, so you can enjoy it wherever and whenever you like!

SERVES 4 Ⓥ ❄
EASY
Syns per serving
Original: Free
Green: Free

Preparation time 10 minutes
Cooking time about 30 minutes

Fry Light
6 spring onions
4 garlic cloves, peeled and finely chopped
400g/14oz wild mushrooms, roughly chopped
4 large eggs
2 tbsp finely chopped fresh sage
2 tbsp pink peppercorns
salt and freshly ground black pepper

To serve
mixed green salad

1. Spray a medium-sized, non-stick frying pan with Fry Light. Place over a high heat and add the spring onions, garlic and mushrooms. Stir-fry for 6–8 minutes.

2. Beat the eggs and stir in the sage and peppercorns. Season well and pour over the mixture in the pan. Cook on a gentle heat for 10–15 minutes, or until the base of the tortilla is set.

3. Place the pan under a medium-hot grill and cook for 4–5 minutes until golden. Allow to rest for 5 minutes before cutting into wedges and serving with a mixed green salad.

aromatic beef with pumpkin

A spicy, warming dish that's ready in almost no time at all. Great for when you're hungry and in a hurry!

SERVES 4 ✳

WORTH THE EFFORT

Syns per serving
Original: Free
Green: 9

Preparation time 15–20 minutes
Cooking time about 20 minutes

Fry Light

2 onions, peeled and cut into thick slices

500g/1lb 2oz pumpkin, peeled and cut into small cubes

500g/1lb 2oz lean beef fillet

60ml/2fl oz soy sauce

1 tsp artificial sweetener

1 bird's-eye chilli, deseeded and chopped

1 tbsp finely shredded ginger

2 tbsp fish sauce

1 tsp ground star anise

1 tsp Chinese five-spice powder

1 tbsp oyster sauce

4 spring onions, shredded

a small handful of sweet basil leaves (optional)

a small handful of mint leaves (optional)

1. Spray a non-stick wok with Fry Light and place over a medium-high heat. Add the onions and pumpkin and stir-fry for about 2–3 minutes. Cover and cook gently for 5–6 minutes, or until just tender.

2. Place the beef between 2 sheets of cling film and beat with a mallet or rolling pin until thin. Cut into thin strips.

3. Put a large frying pan over a medium heat and add the soy sauce, sweetener, chilli, ginger, fish sauce, star anise, five-spice and oyster sauce. Cook and stir for 3–4 minutes.

4. Add the beef strips to the soy mixture and stir-fry over a high heat for 3–4 minutes, or until cooked through. Remove from the heat.

5. Add the pumpkin mixture, spring onions and herbs, if using, to the beef, toss well and serve immediately.

lamb
and root vegetable casserole

This recipe uses black onion seeds, which are also known as nigella or kalonji seeds. They have a distinctive peppery flavour and are available from larger supermarkets.

SERVES 4 ❄

EASY

Syns per serving
Original: Free
Green: 14

Preparation time 20 minutes
Cooking time 1¾ hours

Fry Light

800g/1lb 12oz lean lamb fillet, cut into bite-sized cubes

12 shallots, peeled

8 carrots, peeled and cut into thick batons

400g/14oz swede, peeled and cut into thick batons

10 garlic cloves, unpeeled

1 tsp ground turmeric

2 tsp cumin seeds

2 tsp black onion (nigella) seeds

400ml/14fl oz stock made with chicken or beef Bovril

salt and freshly ground black pepper

To garnish
finely chopped parsley

1. Preheat the oven to 170°C/Gas 3. Spray a large, non-stick frying pan with Fry Light and place over a high heat. Add the lamb and stir-fry for 6–8 minutes or until browned.

2. Remove from the heat and transfer to an ovenproof casserole dish with all the remaining ingredients, apart from the parsley. Season well and bring to the boil over a high heat.

3. Cover tightly and place in the oven for 1½ hours, or until the meat is tender. Remove from the oven and allow to stand, covered, for 10–12 minutes before serving, garnished with the parsley.

wild garlic mushrooms
with polenta

If you can't find wild (field) mushrooms, you can use chestnut or button mushrooms instead. Just make sure they're really fresh.

SERVES 4

WORTH THE EFFORT

Syns per serving
Original: 6½
Green: Free

Preparation time 15 minutes
Cooking time 20 minutes

150g/5oz coarse polenta

1 tbsp finely chopped rosemary leaves

1 tbsp finely chopped sage leaves

8 tbsp finely chopped flat-leaf parsley

1.5 litres/2½ pints boiling chicken stock made with Bovril, or vegetable stock made with Vecon

salt and freshly ground black pepper

Fry Light

800g/1lb 12oz mixed wild mushrooms, thickly sliced if large

3 garlic cloves, peeled and crushed

8 tbsp Quark soft cheese, beaten until smooth

½ tsp crushed dried red chilli

1. Place the polenta in a saucepan along with the rosemary, sage and half the parsley. Set over a medium heat and gradually whisk in the hot stock, stirring continuously. Reduce the heat to low, season well and cook, stirring constantly, until the polenta becomes very thick (this will take about 6–8 minutes). Remove from the heat and keep warm.

2. Spray a large, non-stick frying pan with Fry Light and place over a high heat. Add the mushrooms and garlic and stir-fry for 6–8 minutes.

3. Season well, then stir in the Quark and dried chilli. Stir-fry for 2–3 minutes, until bubbling. Remove from the heat and stir in the remaining parsley.

4. Serve immediately on warmed plates with the polenta.

butternut squash, garlic
and rosemary risotto

These days butternut squash are easy to find in the supermarket: they're pear-shaped, with a pale yellow skin and orange flesh. They're particularly good in this dish, which would make a warming supper on a cold night.

SERVES 4 ⊛
WORTH THE EFFORT
Syns per serving
Green: Free
Original: 11½

Preparation time 15 minutes
Cooking time about 30 minutes

Fry Light

8–10 spring onions, finely chopped

4 garlic cloves, peeled and finely chopped

4 baby leeks, finely sliced

250g/9oz Arborio or risotto rice

400g/14oz butternut squash, cut into small bite-sized pieces

900ml/1½ pints boiling water, or boiling chicken stock made with Bovril

salt and freshly ground black pepper

4 tbsp chopped flat-leaf parsley

1 tbsp finely chopped rosemary leaves

1. Spray a large, non-stick frying pan with Fry Light and place over a medium heat. Add the spring onions, garlic and leeks and stir-fry for 3–4 minutes.

2. Add the rice and squash to the pan and stir-fry for 2–3 minutes. Add a ladleful of the boiling water or stock and cook, stirring, until the liquid is absorbed. Repeat, adding a ladleful at a time, until the stock is used up. The rice should be creamy and al dente (tender but still retaining a bite). This should take about 20–25 minutes.

3. Remove from the heat, season well and stir in the chopped herbs. Ladle into warmed bowls and eat immediately.

> **Butternut squash**
> The squash family is a large one, and its members come in all shapes, sizes and colours. Golden butternut squash has a sweetish, firm flesh that is an ideal match for strong flavours in dishes such as this Butternut Squash, Garlic and Rosemary Risotto. It also mashes and bakes well, so it's a great alternative to potato with roast meat or grilled fish.

quick wild mushroom rice

A lovely filling dish that's great for when time is short. You could boil your own basmati rice if you have the time; this would make the dish Free on a Green day.

SERVES 4 Ⓥ ❄

EASY

Syns per serving

Green: 1½

Original: 9½

Preparation time 10 minutes

Cooking time 15–20 minutes

Fry Light

4 shallots, finely chopped

2 tsp garlic salt

2 tsp cumin seeds

1 red pepper, deseeded and finely diced

400g/14oz wild mushrooms, roughly sliced or chopped

1 tbsp mild curry powder

2 x 250g packs ready-cooked plain basmati rice

salt and freshly ground black pepper

To serve

very low fat natural yogurt (optional)

1. Spray a large, non-stick frying pan with Fry Light and place over a medium heat. Add the shallots and stir-fry for 4–5 minutes.

2. Add the garlic salt, cumin seeds, red pepper and mushrooms to the pan and stir-fry over a high heat for 6–8 minutes.

3. Stir in the curry powder and continue cooking for 2–3 minutes.

4. Add the rice and stir-fry on a high heat for 3–4 minutes, or until piping hot. Remove from the heat, season well and serve with a bowl of yogurt, if wished.

quorn
and vegetable lasagne

A Green day twist to a family favourite that will quickly become as popular as its meaty counterpart!

SERVES 4 Ⓥ ❄

WORTH THE EFFORT

Syns per serving
Green: Free
Original: 7½

Preparation time 20 minutes
Cooking time 50 minutes

Fry Light

300g/11oz Quorn mince

1 red pepper, cut into bite-sized pieces

1 courgette, cut into bite-sized cubes

1 onion, peeled and finely chopped

4 garlic cloves, peeled and crushed

1 x 400g can chopped tomatoes with herbs

2 tsp dried mixed herbs

salt and freshly ground black pepper

400g/14oz very low fat natural fromage frais

110g/4oz Quark soft cheese

1 egg, lightly beaten

a pinch of nutmeg

12 pre-cooked lasagne sheets

1. Spray a large, non-stick frying pan with Fry Light and place over a high heat. Add the Quorn, red pepper, courgette, onion and garlic and stir-fry for 6–8 minutes.

2. Add the tomatoes and dried herbs, season well and cook for 8–10 minutes, stirring often.

3. Meanwhile, put the fromage frais, Quark, egg and nutmeg in a bowl and mix until smooth. Season well.

4. Preheat the oven to 200°C/Gas 6. Spray a medium-sized baking dish with Fry Light. Spoon half the Quorn mixture into the base and top with half the lasagne sheets. Spread half the egg mixture over the pasta and top with the remaining Quorn mixture. Cover with the remaining lasagne sheets and spread with the remaining egg mixture.

5. Bake in the oven for 25–30 minutes, or until the top is golden. Serve immediately.

pasta with artichokes and tomato

Artichoke has a unique flavour that somehow sweetens everything you taste with it or immediately afterwards. Try it and see!

SERVES 4 Ⓥ

EASY

Syns per serving
Green: Free
Original: 15

Preparation time 15 minutes
Cooking time 12–15 minutes

350g/12oz dried pennette or penne

Fry Light

1 onion, peeled and finely chopped

4 garlic cloves, peeled and thinly sliced

2 x 400g canned artichoke hearts in water, rinsed, drained and roughly chopped

2 plum tomatoes, roughly chopped

salt and freshly ground black pepper

1 tbsp finely chopped oregano

1 tbsp finely grated lemon zest

1. Cook the pasta according to the packet instructions.

2. While the pasta is cooking, spray a large, non-stick frying pan with Fry Light and place over a medium heat. Add the onion and garlic and stir-fry for 2–3 minutes.

3. Turn the heat to high, add the artichokes and stir-fry for 3–4 minutes.

4. Add the tomatoes and cook for 3–4 minutes, stirring occasionally. Season well.

5. Drain the pasta and add to the artichoke mixture along with the oregano and lemon zest. Toss well and serve immediately.

macaroni and cauliflower gratin

A great way to use up any leftover pasta and cauliflower (or any other vegetables for that matter). This recipe is also very good with broccoli.

SERVES 4 Ⓥ ❋
WORTH THE EFFORT
Syns per serving
Green: 6
Original: 11½

Preparation time 6–8 minutes
Cooking time about 30 minutes

Fry Light
6 spring onions, thinly sliced
2 garlic cloves, peeled and chopped
450g/1lb cauliflower florets, boiled and drained
400g/14oz cooked macaroni or other short-shape pasta

For the topping
500g/1lb 2oz very low fat natural yogurt
1 tsp Dijon mustard
175g/6oz Cheddar cheese, coarsely grated
2 eggs, lightly beaten
salt and freshly ground black pepper

To serve
grilled vine tomatoes (optional)
steamed green vegetables (optional)

1. Spray a large, non-stick frying pan with Fry Light and place over a high heat. Add the spring onions, garlic and cauliflower and cook, stirring, for 2–3 minutes. Add 100ml/3½fl oz of water to the pan and cook for 4–5 minutes, until the water has been absorbed.

2. Stir in the cooked pasta and toss well. Transfer the mixture to a shallow ovenproof dish. Preheat the oven to 220°C/Gas 7.

3. Mix all the topping ingredients in a bowl. Season well and pour over the pasta mixture. Place in the oven and cook for 15–20 minutes, or until lightly golden and bubbly.

4. Remove from the oven and let stand for 5 minutes before serving. Accompany with grilled vine tomatoes and steamed green vegetables, if wished.

cauliflower curry

A simple dish that's just great served with heaps of steamed rice (2 Syns per 25g/1oz cooked on Original).

SERVES 4 Ⓥ ❄
EASY
Syns per serving
Green: Free
Original: 2

Preparation time 10 minutes
Cooking time about 25 minutes

Fry Light
8 spring onions, cut into 5cm/2in lengths
2 tsp finely grated garlic
2 tsp finely grated ginger
2 tbsp mild curry powder
400g/14oz cauliflower florets
200g/7oz frozen peas
1 red pepper, cut into small squares
500ml/18fl oz passata
1 tsp artificial sweetener
salt and freshly ground black pepper

To serve
3–4 tbsp very low fat natural yogurt
a large handful of chopped mint leaves

1. Spray a large, non-stick frying pan with Fry Light and place over a medium heat. Add the spring onions and stir-fry for 2–3 minutes.

2. Add the garlic, ginger and curry powder and stir-fry for 20–30 seconds. Add the cauliflower, peas and red pepper and stir-fry for 2–3 minutes.

3. Stir in the passata and sweetener and bring to the boil. Cover, lower the heat to medium and cook for 20 minutes, stirring occasionally. Season well.

4. Serve drizzled with the yogurt and garnished with the mint.

Cauliflower

Along with other members of the cruciferous vegetable family, cauliflower provides a variety of micronutrients, but it has less of their distinctive cabbagey aroma. It is a staple of creamy bakes, such as our Macaroni and Cauliflower Gratin (page 128), but raw florets also make a crisp, tasty addition to salads and stir-fries. This vegetable also loves to be spiced up, as in our Cauliflower Curry.

savoy cabbage and potato gratin

The crimped or curly leaves of Savoy cabbage have a mild flavour and are particularly tender. This is a wonderful supper dish for colder autumn nights.

SERVES 4 Ⓥ ❋

WORTH THE EFFORT

Syns per serving

Green: 6

Original: 10½

Preparation time 20 minutes

Cooking time about 1 hour

500g/1lb 2oz potatoes, peeled and roughly chopped

salt and freshly ground black pepper

500g/1lb 2oz Savoy cabbage, finely shredded

Fry Light

6 tbsp very finely chopped flat-leaf parsley

2 eggs, lightly beaten

200g/7oz very low fat natural yogurt

1 tsp paprika

175g/6oz reduced fat Cheddar cheese, coarsely grated

1. Boil the potatoes in a large pan of lightly salted water for 12 minutes. Drain, roughly mash and season well.

2. Meanwhile, boil the cabbage in a large saucepan of lightly salted water for 7–8 minutes. Drain and season well.

3. Preheat the oven to 180°C/Gas 4. Spray a shallow (1.5 litre/2½ pint) ovenproof dish with Fry Light. Spread half the cabbage mixture in the bottom of the dish and put half the potato mixture on top. Repeat with the remaining cabbage and potato. Smooth the top with the back of a spoon.

4. Whisk together the parsley, eggs, yogurt and paprika. Season and pour this mixture over the top layer in the dish. Sprinkle with the cheese and bake in the oven for 45–50 minutes, or until the top is golden brown and set. Serve immediately.

onion, potato, courgette
and tomato bake

Thickly sliced vegetables topped with Parmesan and baked to perfection make a colourful dish that tastes as good as it looks!

SERVES 4 ⓥ ❄

EASY

Syns per serving

With Parmesan

Green: 1

Original: 3

Without Parmesan

Green: Free

Original: 2

Preparation time 10 minutes

Cooking time 30 minutes

2 medium potatoes, peeled and cut into 1cm/½in slices

2 medium onions, peeled and cut into 1cm/½in slices

2 large courgettes, cut into 1cm/½in slices

6 ripe tomatoes, cut into 1cm/½in slices

50ml/2fl oz vegetable stock made with Vecon

4 garlic cloves, peeled and very finely chopped

salt and freshly ground black pepper

To serve

finely chopped parsley

2 tbsp grated Parmesan cheese (optional)

1. Place the potato slices in a large saucepan of lightly salted boiling water and boil for 6–8 minutes, or until just tender. Drain and set aside.

2. Preheat the oven to 200°C/Gas 6. Layer the onions, courgettes, tomatoes and potato slices in a shallow ovenproof dish. Pour over the stock and sprinkle with the garlic. Season well and bake in the oven for 15–20 minutes, or until the vegetables are cooked and bubbling.

3. Before serving, sprinkle with the chopped parsley and Parmesan, if using.

creamy cabbage

There are numerous varieties of cabbage available, but Savoy works best in this tasty side dish. It's great served with roasted meat, fish or poultry.

SERVES 4 Ⓥ ✳
EASY
Syns per serving
Original: Free
Green: Free

Preparation time 10 minutes
Cooking time 15 minutes

700g/1lb 8oz Savoy cabbage, finely shredded

Fry Light

1 tsp wholegrain mustard

150g/5oz very low fat natural fromage frais

salt and freshly ground black pepper

To serve
freshly grated nutmeg

1. Cook the cabbage in a large saucepan of lightly salted boiling water for 8–10 minutes. Drain thoroughly.

2. Spray a large, non-stick wok or frying pan with Fry Light and place over a high heat. Add the cabbage and cook, stirring, for 4–5 minutes.

3. Remove from the heat and stir in the mustard and fromage frais. Season and serve sprinkled with freshly grated nutmeg.

Cabbage

Forget memories of overcooked, soggy cabbage! Curry and chilli taste great on a bed of freshly steamed shredded greens, and raw white and red cabbage are crunchily good in salads such as coleslaw. Darker green varieties are good slow-cooked in bakes, such as Savoy Cabbage and Potato Gratin (page 131), or served with a creamy sauce, as above.

red cabbage
with apple and cranberries

The combination of cabbage and fruit makes this a lovely warming side dish that goes well with roasted meats.

SERVES 4 Ⓥ ❄

EASY

Syns per serving

Original: 1½

Green: 1½

Preparation time 20 minutes

Cooking time about 1 hour

Fry Light

2 red onions, peeled and thinly sliced

1 small red cabbage (about 1kg/2lb 4oz), finely shredded

2 red apples, cored and sliced

110g/4oz cranberries

2 tbsp red wine vinegar

4 tbsp artificial sweetener

1 cinnamon stick

4 cloves

2 star anise

salt and freshly ground black pepper

1. Spray a heavy-based casserole dish with Fry Light and place over a medium heat. Add the onions and cook for 10 minutes or until softened.

2. Stir in the remaining ingredients, season and cover tightly. Cook over a gentle heat for 50 minutes, stirring occasionally, until the cabbage is just soft. Remove from the heat and serve.

blackberry and pear
crumbles

Fruit crumble is the ultimate comfort food: topped with creamy custard (1 Syn per 2 level tbsp), it's sheer bliss in a dish!

SERVES 4 Ⓥ ❄
EASY
Syns per serving
Original: 9
Green: 9

Preparation time 20 minutes
Cooking time 15–20 minutes

2 pears, peeled, cored and cut into bite-sized pieces
400g/14oz blackberries
artificial sweetener, to taste

For the crumble topping
50g/2oz self-raising wholemeal flour
1 tsp cinnamon
¼ tsp allspice
4 tbsp low fat spread
2 tbsp soft brown sugar

To serve
canned low fat custard (optional)
very low fat natural yogurt (optional)

1. Place the fruit and sweetener in a large bowl, add 4 tbsp water and mix well. Divide between 4 individual ovenproof pie dishes (or you can use a single large one).

2. Preheat the oven to 190°C/Gas 5. Sift the flour, cinnamon and allspice into a bowl and rub in the spread with your fingers until the mixture resembles breadcrumbs. Spoon this over the fruit, then sprinkle with the sugar. Bake for 15–20 minutes, or until bubbling and the topping is crisp and golden.

3. Serve immediately with low fat custard or very low fat natural yogurt, if wished.

Blackberries
Glossy British blackberries are ripe for harvesting in early autumn, and are available in bags of frozen mixed berries too. The sweet fruits are rich in vitamin C and other antioxidants, and in fibre – but enjoy them for the depth of flavour they add to fruit compotes, or as a partner in warming autumn desserts, such as these Blackberry and Pear Crumbles.

cranberry jellies

For a special occasion, use a dry sparkling white or rosé wine instead of the soda – just add 2 Syns per serving!

SERVES 4 Ⓥ

WORTH THE EFFORT

Syns per serving
Original: 1
Green: 1

Preparation time 10 minutes plus chilling
Cooking time 8–10 minutes

250ml/9fl oz Ocean Spray Light Cranberry Classic Juice Drink

150g/5oz fresh cranberries

6–8 tbsp artificial sweetener (or more to taste)

15g/½oz powdered gelatine

200ml/7fl oz chilled soda water

To garnish

very low fat natural fromage frais

mint leaves

1. Pour the cranberry juice drink into a saucepan and add the cranberries and sweetener. Bring to the boil, lower the heat and simmer gently for 5 minutes, or until the cranberries have softened. Check the flavour and add more sweetener if you wish.

2. Strain the cranberry mixture through a fine sieve into a bowl, pressing the cranberries with the back of a spoon to extract all the juice. Return the liquid to the pan and bring to the boil. Remove from the heat and sprinkle over the gelatine. Stir to dissolve and allow to cool.

3. When cool, add the soda water, then pour the mixture into 4 chilled dessert glasses. Place in the fridge for 5-6 hours, or until set.

4. Serve the jellies garnished with a spoonful of fromage frais and some mint leaves.

apple posset

Cooking apples work best in this recipe. Bramleys are probably the best known, but other varieties would work equally well.

SERVES 4 Ⓥ

EASY

Syns per serving

Original: 3

Green: 3

Preparation time 5 minutes plus chilling

Cooking time 12–15 minutes

600g/1lb 6oz apples, peeled, cored and chopped

2 tbsp artificial sweetener

1 tbsp lemon juice

2 large egg whites

To garnish

apple slices

mint leaves

1. Place the apples in a saucepan with 150ml/5fl oz of water and a tablespoon of the sweetener. Bring to the boil, reduce the heat and cook gently for 10–12 minutes, until tender. Transfer to a food processor and blend until smooth. Sieve this mixture into a bowl. Allow to cool, then stir in the lemon juice.

2. Whisk the egg whites until softly peaked, then gradually whisk in the remaining sweetener until the mixture is shiny and stiff.

3. Carefully fold the egg whites into the apple mixture until well combined, then spoon into 4 chilled dessert bowls. Place in the fridge for 2–3 hours.

4. Serve chilled, garnished with apple slices and mint leaves.

Apples

Endlessly versatile, apples can add a sweet crunch to hearty salads, be used to make tangy sauces, stuffings and vegetable bakes, or lend themselves to British dessert classics, such as pies, crumbles or our light Apple Posset. From super-sweet red varieties to tart green 'cookers', there's an apple to suit every meal and mood – and as a source of vitamin C and soluble fibre, they're always a healthy choice.

winter

WHAT'S IN SEASON
beef ~ carrots ~ chillies ~ haddock
oysters ~ parsnips ~ pomegranates ~
swede ~ turkey ~ turnips

borscht

Although traditionally served hot, this soup is also good when cold; just place in the fridge and chill for a couple of hours before serving.

SERVES 4 ❄

EASY

Syns per serving
Original: Free
Green: Free

Preparation time 20 minutes
Cooking time 4 hours

450g/1lb uncooked beetroot, peeled and grated

1 large carrot, finely diced

1 onion, peeled and chopped

110g/4oz white cabbage, shredded

1 tsp artificial sweetener

1 bay leaf

1.5 litres/2½ pints water, or chicken stock made with Bovril

salt and freshly ground black pepper

To serve
very low fat natural fromage frais

chopped chives

1. Preheat the oven to 140°C/Gas 1. Place all the ingredients in an ovenproof casserole dish, cover tightly and cook in the oven for 4 hours, or until all the vegetables are tender. Remove the bay leaf and discard.

2. Transfer the vegetable mixture to a food processor and blend until smooth. Add seasoning and blend again. To serve, ladle into warmed bowls and garnish with a spoonful of fromage frais and a few chopped chives.

lentil
broth

A lovely warming broth of lentils, onions, carrots and celery: it's just made for a winter's day lunch!

SERVES 4 Ⓥ ❄

WORTH THE EFFORT

Syns per serving

Green: Free

Original: 11

Preparation time 30 minutes plus soaking

Cooking time about 40 minutes

300g/11oz split red lentils

Fry Light

2 onions, peeled and finely chopped

3 carrots, peeled and finely chopped

4 sticks celery, finely chopped

2 garlic cloves, peeled and finely diced

1 bay leaf

3 sprigs of parsley

1.5 litres/2½ pints water, or vegetable stock made with Vecon

salt and freshly ground black pepper

To garnish

4 tbsp very low fat natural fromage frais

chopped parsley

1. Wash the lentils in a sieve under cold running water. Tip into a bowl and cover with hot water. Leave to soak for 30 minutes.

2. Spray a large, non-stick saucepan with Fry Light and place over a medium heat. Add the vegetables and garlic and stir-fry for 10 minutes, or until softened.

3. Drain the lentils and add to the pan with the herbs and the water or stock. Bring to the boil, then lower the heat and simmer gently for 30 minutes, skimming off any scum that comes to the surface.

4. Remove the bay leaf and parsley, transfer the mixture to a food processor and blend until smooth.

5. Return the soup to the pan, season well and reheat before serving. Ladle into warmed bowls and garnish each one with a tablespoon of fromage frais and some chopped parsley.

mixed bean salad

Using canned mixed beans helps make this a really quick and easy dish to prepare. They're available in all good supermarkets.

SERVES 4 Ⓥ

EASY

Syns per serving

Green: Free

Original: 6

Preparation time 5 minutes

Cooking time 5 minutes

300g/11oz French beans, trimmed

300g/11oz sugar snap peas, trimmed

600g/1lb 6oz canned mixed beans, rinsed and drained

1 red onion, peeled and finely chopped

2 plum tomatoes roughly chopped

For the dressing

6 tbsp fat-free vinaigrette dressing

2 garlic cloves, peeled and crushed

1 tsp Dijon mustard

salt and freshly ground black pepper

To garnish

lemon zest (optional)

1. Bring a large pan of lightly salted water to the boil and add the French beans and sugar snap peas. Bring back to the boil, then drain and refresh under cold running water. Drain again and place in a salad bowl.

2. Add the canned beans, onion and tomatoes to the bowl and mix well.

3. Combine all the dressing ingredients, season and mix well. Pour over the bean mixture, toss thoroughly and garnish with lemon zest before serving, if desired.

smoked salmon
soufflés

This recipe uses that perennial favourite, smoked salmon. It's a perfect dinner-party starter!

SERVES 4 ❋

WORTH THE EFFORT

Syns per serving
With Parmesan
Original: 1
Green: 4½

Without Parmesan
Original: Free
Green: 3½

Preparation time 20 minutes
Cooking time 30 minutes

Fry Light

50g/2oz finely chopped leek or spring onions

200g/7oz smoked salmon, roughly chopped

8 tbsp finely chopped dill

2 tbsp crushed pink peppercorns

3 large eggs, separated

salt and freshly ground black pepper

2 tbsp grated Parmesan cheese (optional)

1. Preheat the oven to 190°C/Gas 5. Spray a large, non-stick frying pan with Fry Light and add the leeks or spring onions. Stir-fry over a gentle heat for 5–6 minutes, or until softened.

2. Transfer to a bowl and leave to cool. When cool, stir in the smoked salmon, dill and peppercorns.

3. Lightly beat the egg yolks and add to the salmon mixture. Season and stir in the Parmesan, if using, and mix well.

4. In a separate bowl, beat the egg whites until softly peaked. Fold into the salmon mixture using a metal spoon, then divide between 4 individual, lightly greased soufflé dishes (or a single medium-sized dish). Place on a baking sheet and bake in the oven for 20–25 minutes, or until risen and golden. Serve immediately.

bouillabaisse

This is a wonderfully flavoursome fish stew, and the great thing about it is that you can use any combination of fish you like.

SERVES 4 ❄

WORTH THE EFFORT

Syns per serving
Original: Free
Green: 13½

Preparation time 5–6 minutes
Cooking time 8–10 minutes

Fry Light

1 leek, white parts only, finely diced

4 garlic cloves, peeled and thinly sliced

2 tsp fennel seeds

½ tsp dried red chilli flakes

4 ripe tomatoes, roughly chopped

1 tsp artificial sweetener

1.5 litres/2½ pints chicken stock made with Bovril

1 fresh bouquet garni (2 thyme sprigs, 1 parsley sprig and 2 bay leaves tied with string)

1.5 kg/3lb 6oz mixed fish, such as cod, haddock and prawns, cut into large pieces

salt and freshly ground black pepper

cayenne pepper

To garnish

finely chopped parsley

1. Spray a large, non-stick saucepan with Fry Light and place over a medium heat. Add the leeks, garlic, fennel seeds and chilli and stir-fry for 2–3 minutes.

2. Add the tomatoes, sweetener, stock and bouquet garni and bring to the boil. Stir in the fish, bring back to the boil, then lower the heat and simmer gently for 5–6 minutes, or until the fish is cooked through. Season well with salt, pepper and cayenne pepper.

3. To serve, divide the fish between 4 large, shallow bowls. Strain the soup and ladle it over the fish. Garnish with the parsley and serve immediately.

oysters
kilpatrick

One of life's luxuries, oysters evoke passionate feelings – you either love them or hate them. If you're not a fan, this recipe could change your mind!

SERVES 4

WORTH THE EFFORT

Syns per serving
Original: 1½
Green: 4½

Preparation time 15 minutes
Cooking time 8–12 minutes

Fry Light

3 lean bacon rashers, finely chopped

1 shallot, peeled and finely chopped

2 tbsp fresh wholemeal breadcrumbs

12 oysters, opened and top shell discarded

rock salt (optional)

1 tbsp Worcestershire sauce

1 garlic clove, peeled and crushed

4 tbsp very low fat natural fromage frais

salt and freshly ground black pepper

To serve

lemon wedges

Tabasco sauce (optional)

1. Spray a large, non-stick frying pan with Fry Light and place over a medium heat. Add the bacon and shallot and stir-fry for 5–6 minutes.

2. Add the breadcrumbs and stir-fry for 2–3 minutes. Remove from the heat and set aside.

3. Arrange the opened oysters on a baking sheet (you can line the sheet with rock salt to keep the half-shells stable). Mix together the Worcestershire sauce, garlic and fromage frais and divide it between the 12 oysters. Season well and top each one with the breadcrumb mixture.

4. Place the oysters under a medium-hot grill and cook for 1–2 minutes. Serve immediately with lemon wedges and Tabasco sauce, if using.

tip

To open an oyster, wrap your holding hand in a tea towel and grasp an oyster, flat side up, in your palm. Insert a short, wide-bladed knife under the hinge and push it into the oyster. Jerk the blade upwards and the shells should come apart. Take care not to lose the liquid inside the oyster.

Oysters

Traditionally served raw with lemon juice and a dash of Tabasco, oysters earned their aphrodisiac reputation because of their very high zinc content, which is important in the male reproductive system. Our recipe, Oysters Kilpatrick, is a Christmas and New Year favourite, and teams oysters with bacon and a creamy yet tangy sauce.

baked haddock
with tomatoes and spinach

The flavour of the succulent haddock in this dish marries well with the spinach and juicy tomatoes.

SERVES 4

WORTH THE EFFORT

Syns per serving
Original: 3½
Green: 6

Preparation time 15 minutes
Cooking time about 15 minutes

400g/14oz spinach, roughly chopped

salt and freshly ground black pepper

Fry Light

4 x 250g/9oz haddock fillets

4 ripe plum tomatoes, finely chopped

400g/14oz very low fat natural yogurt

3 egg yolks

½ tsp nutmeg

2 tbsp grated Cheddar cheese (optional)

4 tbsp dried wholemeal breadcrumbs

1. Preheat the oven to 200°C/Gas 6. Boil the spinach for 2–3 minutes, drain thoroughly and finely chop. Season well.

2. Lightly spray a medium, shallow ovenproof dish with Fry Light. Spread the spinach evenly in the bottom of the dish, then place the haddock on top in a single layer. Season well, scatter with the chopped tomatoes and place in the oven for 6–8 minutes.

3. Meanwhile, mix together the yogurt, egg yolks and nutmeg, and season well.

4. Remove the fish from the oven and spoon the yogurt mixture evenly over each fish portion. Sprinkle with the Cheddar, if using, and the breadcrumbs.

5. Place under a medium-hot grill for 4–5 minutes, or until the sauce is golden and bubbly and the fish is cooked through. Serve immediately.

Haddock

Winter is the best time to eat firm-fleshed white fish, such as haddock, which is a member of the cod family. To make the most of its delicate flavour, grill it and serve with lemon and parsley, or try our tasty recipe for Baked Haddock with Tomatoes and Spinach – it's colourful and very healthy because haddock is low in fat and high in B vitamins.

steak and kidney pies

The filling for these pies can be made the day before you need it and kept in the fridge. It's then quick work to fill the pie dishes, top with the pastry and bake!

SERVES 4 ❋

WORTH THE EFFORT

Syns per serving
Original: 11½
Green: 22½

Preparation time 20 minutes
Cooking time about 2¾ hours

Fry Light

500g/1lb 2oz lean steak, cut into 2.5cm/1in cubes

400g/14oz button mushrooms, quartered or halved

150g/5oz ox kidney, trimmed and cut into very small cubes

2 onions, peeled, halved and sliced

2 tbsp Worcestershire sauce

1 tsp finely chopped thyme leaves

500ml/18fl oz beef stock made with Bovril

1 tbsp gravy granules

salt and freshly ground black pepper

200g/7oz puff pastry

2 eggs, lightly beaten

1. Preheat the oven to 140°C/Gas 1. Spray a large, heavy-based, non-stick casserole dish with Fry Light and place over a high heat. Add the steak and stir-fry until brown and sealed.

2. Add the mushrooms, kidney and onions and stir-fry over a high heat for 6–8 minutes.

3. Stir in the Worcestershire sauce, thyme, stock and gravy granules, season well and bring to the boil. Cover tightly, then place in the oven for 2 hours, or until the meat is tender. Remove from the oven and increase the heat to 220°C/Gas 7.

4. Divide the meat and its juices between 4 individual pie dishes or rimmed ovenproof soup bowls with diameters of about 13cm/5in.

5. Flour a work surface, roll out the pastry and cut 4 'lids' to fit the top of each pie dish. Brush the rim of each dish with water, position the pastry lids, then press around the edges to seal. Make a hole in the centre of each lid and brush the surface with the beaten eggs.

6. Place the pies in the oven and bake for 20–25 minutes, or until the pastry is risen and golden. Serve immediately.

daube of beef

A hearty, warming stew of beef and chunky vegetables that's just perfect for supper on a cold winter's night!

SERVES 4 ❊
EASY
Syns per serving
Original: Free
Green: 12

Preparation time 15–20 minutes
Cooking time 2¼ hours

Fry Light
700g/1lb 8oz lean stewing beef, cut into bite-sized pieces
2 garlic cloves, peeled and crushed
2 onions, peeled and roughly chopped
3 carrots, peeled and roughly chopped
1 medium turnip, cubed
600ml/22fl oz beef stock made with Bovril
salt and freshly ground black pepper
2 tsp dried mixed herbs

To garnish
chopped parsley

1. Preheat the oven to 170°C/Gas 3. Spray a large, non-stick frying pan with Fry Light and place over a medium heat. Add the meat and stir-fry until brown on all sides.

2. Transfer the meat to a medium casserole dish with the garlic, onions, carrots, turnip and stock. Season well and add the dried mixed herbs. Cover tightly and cook in the oven for 2 hours.

3. Serve piping hot, sprinkled with the chopped parsley.

Beef

There's nothing like a warming beef stew when it's cold outside, and our Daube of Beef, based on a traditional French recipe, will not disappoint. Lean beef is only 5 per cent fat and contains valuable minerals, especially iron and zinc, so it's a deliciously healthy choice stir-fried with ginger and onions, spiced up into a curry, or served simply as a big juicy steak.

pork stroganoff

The gentle cooking of the pork gives it a tenderness that makes this stroganoff something really special.

SERVES 4 ✳
WORTH THE EFFORT
Syns per serving
Original: Free
Green: 10½

Preparation time 10 minutes
Cooking time 1¾–2 hours

Fry Light

12 shallots, peeled and halved

2 garlic cloves, peeled and finely chopped

1 bay leaf

2 tsp paprika

800g/1lb 12oz lean pork, cut into bite-sized pieces

2 red peppers, cut into bite-sized pieces

1 x 400g can chopped tomatoes

200ml/7fl oz beef stock made with Bovril

salt and freshly ground black pepper

200g/7oz very low fat natural fromage frais

chopped parsley

1. Spray a large, non-stick frying pan with Fry Light and place over a medium heat. Add the shallots and stir-fry for 2–3 minutes, until lightly brown.

2. Add the garlic and bay leaf and stir for 2–3 minutes.

3. Add the paprika, pork and peppers and stir-fry for 6–8 minutes. Add the tomatoes and stock and bring to the boil. Season well and cover tightly. Lower the heat and cook gently for 1½–2 hours, stirring occasionally, or until the pork is meltingly tender.

4. Remove from the heat and stir in the fromage frais and chopped parsley before serving.

slow-simmered ham hocks

A simple and flavoursome way to cook ham that would be great served with Glazed Turnips with Chervil (opposite) or Free vegetables of your choice.

SERVES 4 ❀

EASY

Syns per serving
Original: Free
Green: 36

Preparation time 10 minutes
plus overnight soaking
Cooking time 2½–3 hours

2 ham hocks, each weighing about 1kg/2lb 4oz

1 litre/1¾ pints chicken stock made with Bovril

2 onions, peeled and halved

2 large carrots, peeled and cut into large chunks

4 sticks celery, cut into 3cm/1¼in pieces

2 tsp black peppercorns

1 bay leaf

a few sprigs of thyme

1. Soak the ham hocks in cold water overnight. Rinse and place in a heavy-based, large saucepan with the stock, vegetables, peppercorns and herbs. Add enough water to cover them well.

2. Bring to the boil, lower the heat and simmer gently for 2½–3 hours, or until the meat is very tender and almost coming away from the bone. Check the water level now and again, topping up if necessary.

3. When the hocks are done, drain and discard the vegetables and any remaining liquid. Trim all visible fat from the hocks.

4. To serve, remove all the meat from the bones and divide between 4 warmed plates. Serve with Glazed Turnips.

glazed turnips with chervil

Turnips have a peppery flavour that's complemented by the chervil. This dish would be a great accompaniment to the Slow-simmered Ham Hocks (opposite).

SERVES 4 Ⓥ ❅

EASY

Syns per serving
Original: 1½
Green: 1½

Preparation time 15 minutes
Cooking time 12–15 minutes

800g/1lb 12oz young turnips, peeled and trimmed

2 tsp artificial sweetener

salt and freshly ground black pepper

2 tbsp low fat spread

2 tbsp finely chopped chervil

1. If the turnips are small, leave them whole; if large, cut them into halves or quarters. Place them in a pan and add just enough boiling water to cover. Add the sweetener and season well. Bring to the boil, reduce the heat to medium and cook for 7–8 minutes, or until tender.

2. Drain the turnips and return to the pan with the low fat spread and chervil. Toss well and serve immediately.

Turnips

Versatile and high in filling power, the turnip is an underrated root veg. It has a nutty, savoury taste and can be mashed, stewed or braised, as in our Glazed Turnips with Chervil. Also, green turnip tops can be boiled as an unusual savoury side dish. Turnips are a good source of vitamin C, and of fibre, which helps the digestive system.

angel hair pasta
with chilli and coriander

Cappellini pasta is very fine, which is why it's known as 'angel hair'. This dish would be great eaten for lunch or as a main course meal.

SERVES 4 ⓥ

EASY

Syns per serving

With Parmesan

Green: 1

Original: 23½

Without Parmesan

Original: 22½

Green: Free

Preparation time 6–8 minutes

Cooking time 10 minutes

500g/1lb 2oz dried angel hair pasta

Fry Light

6 spring onions, finely chopped

2 garlic cloves, peeled and finely sliced

2 plum tomatoes, finely chopped

1–2 red chillies, deseeded and finely diced

a large handful of chopped coriander leaves

salt and freshly ground black pepper

To serve

2 tbsp grated Parmesan cheese (optional)

1. Cook the pasta according to the packet instructions. Drain, set aside and keep warm.

2. While the pasta is cooking, spray a large, non-stick frying pan with Fry Light and add the onions and garlic. Stir and cook for 3–4 minutes, then add the tomatoes and chillies. Stir-fry for a further 2–3 minutes.

3. Remove from the heat and stir in the coriander and pasta. Season well, and serve sprinkled with Parmesan, if using.

Chillies

There are umpteen varieties of chilli, all of them great winter warmers. Generally, the smaller and darker the chilli, the hotter it is. Capsaicin, the heat-generating compound in chillies, has all sorts of health benefits, so make the most of this ingredient in Indian and Thai curries, Mexican chilli con carne, Chinese stir-fries, or simple suppers with a kick of heat, such as our Angel Hair Pasta with Chilli and Coriander.

mixed bean stew with feta

Traditionally, dried butter beans are used in this stew. However, as these need overnight soaking and long cooking, we use canned beans here for a quicker version.

SERVES 4 ⓥ ❄

WORTH THE EFFORT

Syns per serving

Green: 5½

Original: 11½

Preparation time 15 minutes

Cooking time about 1 hour

Fry Light

1 onion, peeled and finely chopped

2 garlic cloves, peeled and crushed

1 x 400g can chopped tomatoes

2 bay leaves

2 tbsp finely chopped parsley

4 tbsp finely chopped dill

salt and freshly ground black pepper

1 tsp paprika

½ tsp artificial sweetener

600g/1lb 6oz canned mixed beans, such as butter beans, cannellini beans and red kidney beans, rinsed and drained

175g/6oz feta cheese, cut into chunky cubes

1. Spray a large frying pan with Fry Light and place over a medium heat. Add the onion and stir-fry for 5–6 minutes, or until soft.

2. Add the garlic, tomatoes and 450ml/16fl oz of water. Stir in the bay leaves, parsley and half the dill. Season well, then stir in the paprika and sweetener and bring to the boil. Partially cover the pan, lower the heat and simmer gently for 25–30 minutes, until the sauce has thickened.

3. Add the beans and simmer gently for another 10–12 minutes.

4. Add the feta to the pan and cook gently for 3–4 minutes. Serve in warmed bowls, scattered with the remaining dill.

braised red cabbage

A traditional seasonal side dish that's the perfect partner to a host of hot and cold meat and poultry dishes!

SERVES 4 ⓥ ❋

EASY

Syns per serving
Original: Free
Green: Free

Preparation time 15 minutes
Cooking time 3 hours

Fry Light

1kg/2lb 4oz red cabbage, finely shredded

400g/14oz red onions, peeled and finely sliced

salt and freshly ground black pepper

1 tbsp ground ginger

4 tbsp artificial sweetener

6 tbsp red wine vinegar

1. Preheat the oven to 150°C/Gas 5. Spray a medium-sized, ovenproof casserole dish with Fry Light and layer the cabbage and onions in it, seasoning well. Spray the mixture with Fry Light.

2. Mix together the ginger, sweetener and vinegar and pour over the cabbage mixture. Cover tightly and cook in the oven for 3 hours, stirring occasionally. Check the seasoning and serve.

kedgeree

We've used lentils and vegetables in place of fish in this recipe to make this a fabulous Green day treat.

SERVES 4 Ⓥ ❄

WORTH THE EFFORT

Syns per serving

Green: Free

Original: 13

Preparation time 20 minutes

Cooking time about 45 minutes

Fry Light

1 onion, peeled and finely chopped

2 garlic cloves, peeled and finely chopped

1 tsp finely grated ginger

2 tsp cumin seeds

2 tsp mild curry powder

1 tsp ground cinnamon

½ tsp crushed cardamom seeds

1 clove

110g/4oz dried split lentils, rinsed and drained

200g/7oz brown basmati rice, rinsed and drained

1 carrot, peeled and cut into 1cm/½in dice

110g/4oz fine green beans, cut into 1cm/½in lengths

freshly ground black pepper

3 tbsp finely chopped coriander leaves

To serve

4 eggs, boiled and halved

200g/7oz very low fat natural yogurt, whisked

chilli powder or paprika

1. Spray a large, heavy-based saucepan with Fry Light and place over a medium heat. Add the onion, garlic and ginger and stir-fry for 3–4 minutes.

2. Stir in the cumin seeds, curry powder, cinnamon, cardamom seeds and clove and stir-fry for 1 minute.

3. Add the lentils, rice, carrot and beans and mix well. Pour in 700ml/24fl oz of water and bring to the boil. Lower the heat, cover and cook gently for about 30–40 minutes, or until all the liquid has been absorbed and the mixture is slightly sticky (do not be tempted to uncover the saucepan during this time).

4. Remove the pan from the heat and allow to stand, covered, for 10–12 minutes.

5. Fluff up the lentil mixture with a fork and season with pepper. Stir in the coriander and spoon into 4 shallow dishes. Garnish with the eggs and serve immediately with the yogurt sprinkled with chilli powder or paprika.

tomato
and carrot rice

This dish contains lots of textures – juicy tomatoes, crunchy peppers and carrots, and fluffy rice – and it's ready in minutes!

SERVES 4 Ⓥ ❋
EASY
Syns per serving
Green: Free
Original: 11

Preparation time 5 minutes
Cooking time about 15 minutes

Fry Light

1 onion, peeled and finely chopped

1 garlic clove, peeled and finely chopped

½ red pepper, finely diced

6 plum tomatoes, roughly chopped

3 large carrots, peeled and coarsely grated

200g/7oz fresh or frozen peas

500g/1lb 2oz cooked white or brown basmati rice

4 tbsp finely chopped parsley

salt and freshly ground black pepper

1. Spray a large, non-stick frying pan with Fry Light and place over a medium heat. Add the onion, garlic and red pepper and stir-fry for 4–5 minutes.

2. Stir in the tomatoes, carrots and peas, increase the heat to high and stir-fry for 3–4 minutes.

3. Add the rice and mix well. Stir-fry for 3–4 minutes, until piping hot. Remove from the heat, stir in the chopped parsley, season well and serve.

leek, carrot
and parsnip purée

Parsnips are sweet, but have a distinctly earthy flavour too. This recipe is 'mash' with a difference, and bound to become a regular on the menu!

SERVES 4 Ⓥ ❄
EASY
Syns per serving
Green: Free
Original: 4½

Preparation time 15 minutes
Cooking time 25 minutes

500g/1lb 2oz parsnips, peeled and roughly chopped

500g/1lb 2oz carrots, peeled and roughly chopped

2 tsp ground ginger

Fry Light

2 leeks, finely sliced

200g/7oz very low fat natural fromage frais

salt and freshly ground black pepper

To garnish
chopped flat-leaf parsley

1. Boil the parsnips and carrots in a large saucepan of lightly salted water until tender. Drain, return to the saucepan, add the ginger and roughly mash.

2. While the vegetables are cooking, spray a large, non-stick frying pan with Fry Light and place over a medium heat. Add the leeks and stir-fry for 10–12 minutes, or until softened.

3. Add the leeks to the carrot and parsnip mixture, then stir in the fromage frais and seasoning. Garnish with the parsley just before serving.

Carrots
Being both nutty and sweet, carrots are used in everything from hotpots to cakes, and have a special place in British cooking. Rich in beta carotene (which really can help you see in the dark), they are tasty eaten raw with dips or in salads, but are more nutritious cooked in stews or with roasts, or turned into a delicious mash, such as our Leek, Carrot and Parsnip Purée.

roasted spiced beetroot

If you've only ever eaten beetroot cold and pickled, this lovely recipe could convert you to eating it roasted and spiced!

SERVES 4 Ⓥ ❉

WORTH THE EFFORT

Syns per serving
Original: Free
Green: Free

Preparation time 10 minutes
Cooking time 35–40 minutes

1kg/2lb 4oz fresh beetroot, peeled

Fry Light

150g/5oz very low fat natural yogurt

25g/1oz fresh coriander, finely chopped

1 tsp ground cumin

1 tsp toasted cumin seeds

salt and freshly ground black pepper

50g/2oz wild rocket leaves

2 tbsp toasted nigella seeds

1. Preheat the oven to 200°C/Gas 6. Cut the beetroot into bite-sized wedges. Place on a non-stick baking sheet and spray with Fry Light. Roast in the oven for 35–40 minutes, or until just tender. Remove and allow to cool.

2. Meanwhile, place the yogurt, coriander, ground cumin and cumin seeds in a food processor. Process for a few minutes until smooth, then transfer to a bowl and season well. Add the cooled beetroot, season well and toss to coat evenly.

3. To serve, divide the rocket leaves between 4 large plates, top with the beetroot mixture and sprinkle over the nigella seeds.

tip

To toast seeds, place them in a dry frying pan and heat for a minute or two, stirring constantly, until they give off a rich aroma.

cheesy potato and tomato pie

This quick and easy recipe would make a great lunch simply served with heaps of baked beans.

SERVES 4 Ⓥ ❋
EASY
Syns per serving
Green: 6
Original: 9

Preparation time 10 minutes
Cooking time 30 minutes

3 medium potatoes, peeled and cut into 1cm/½in slices

2 medium onions, peeled and cut into 1cm/½in slices

6 ripe tomatoes, cut into 1cm/½in slices

60ml/2fl oz vegetable stock made with Vecon

175g/6oz reduced fat Cheddar cheese, coarsely grated

4 garlic cloves, peeled and very finely chopped

salt and freshly ground black pepper

To garnish
finely chopped parsley

1. Place the potato slices in a large saucepan of lightly salted boiling water and boil for 6–8 minutes, or until just tender. Drain and set aside.

2. Preheat the oven to 200°C/Gas 6. Place the onions, tomatoes and potatoes randomly in a shallow ovenproof dish, or in separate layers if you wish. Pour over the stock and sprinkle the cheese and garlic on the top. Season well.

3. Place in the oven and bake for 15–20 minutes, or until the vegetables are cooked and bubbling. Garnish with the chopped parsley before serving.

fantail potato roasties

This way of cooking potatoes comes from Sweden, where they are known as Hasselback potatoes. Whatever you call them, they're a fabulous alternative to plain roast potatoes!

SERVES 4 Ⓥ ❋
EASY
Syns per serving
Green: Free
Original: 9

Preparation time 15 minutes
Cooking time about 1 hour

1kg/2lb 4oz medium potatoes, such as King Edwards or Maris Piper, scrubbed
Fry Light
sea salt and freshly ground black pepper
8–10 small sprigs of rosemary

1. Preheat the oven to 220°C/Gas 7. Using a sharp knife, slice into each potato widthways at 5mm/¼in intervals, going just three-quarters of the way through the flesh (see tip below).

2. Place the potatoes on a non-stick baking tray and spray generously with Fry Light. Season with the sea salt and pepper. Scatter over the rosemary sprigs and cook for about 1 hour, or until the potatoes are crisp and cooked all the way through. Remove from the oven and serve.

tip
If you push a skewer through the base of the potato along its length, it will stop you cutting all the way through the flesh.

colcannon cakes

These are great just eaten on their own as a snack, but they would also make a terrific lunch served with Quorn sausages and mushy peas.

SERVES 4 Ⓥ ❄

EASY

Syns per serving

Green: Free

Original: 9

Preparation time 10 minutes plus chilling

Cooking time 30 minutes

1kg/2lb 4oz Desirée potatoes, peeled and roughly chopped

400g/14oz green cabbage, finely shredded

1 large egg yolk

6 spring onions, finely sliced

salt and freshly ground black pepper

Fry Light

1. Boil the potatoes in a large saucepan of lightly salted water until just tender. Drain thoroughly, return to the saucepan and add the cabbage. Set aside to cool.

2. When cool, add the egg yolk and spring onions. Season well and mix thoroughly. Cover and place this mixture in the fridge for 3–4 hours.

3. When ready to cook, preheat the oven to 220°C/Gas 7. Line a non-stick baking sheet with baking parchment. Divide the potato mixture into 8 portions and shape each into a large 'cake' about 2cm/¾in thick and 5cm/2in wide. Place the cakes on the prepared baking sheet and spray with Fry Light. Bake in the oven for 12–15 minutes, or until warmed through and slightly browned.

honey-roasted
roots

A twist on honey-roasted parsnips – we've added carrots, potatoes and butternut squash to the mix, and the result is just wonderful.

SERVES 4 ⓥ ❋
EASY
Syns per serving
Green: 1½
Original: 8½

Preparation time 20 minutes
Cooking time 30 minutes

400g/14oz parsnips
400g/14oz carrots
400g/14oz potatoes
400g/14oz butternut squash
Fry Light
2 tbsp runny honey
4–5 small sprigs of rosemary
salt and freshly ground black pepper

1. Preheat the oven to 220°C/Gas 7. Peel all the vegetables and cut them into 2.5cm/1in pieces. Blanch the vegetables in a large saucepan of lightly salted boiling water for 5–6 minutes, drain well and transfer to a large, non-stick roasting tin.

2. Spray the vegetables with Fry Light, drizzle over the honey and sprinkle with the rosemary. Season well and toss to mix evenly.

3. Place in the oven and roast for 20–25 minutes, or until golden and tender.

Parsnips
Although parsnips are related to carrots and are similarly sweet, they have a distinct earthy flavour. Best enjoyed in the depths of winter, the natural sweetness takes on a deliciously nutty flavour when parsnips are slow roasted. They go well with other root vegetables, particularly when mashed or puréed (page 169), and are just perfect for our Honey-roasted Roots recipe.

tabbouleh
with pomegranate, clementine and parsley

Tabbouleh is a salad made with 'cooked' bulgur wheat that's mixed with lots of chopped vegetables or fruit, and then seasoned. Simple!

SERVES 4 Ⓥ

EASY

Syns per serving

Green: Free

Original: 7½

Preparation time 20 minutes

175g/6oz bulgur wheat

10 clementines, peeled and sliced into thin circles

seeds from 1 pomegranate

a small handful of roughly chopped flat-leaf parsley

4 tbsp finely chopped mint leaves

salt and freshly ground black pepper

1. Place the bulgur wheat in a large heatproof bowl and pour over 350ml/12fl oz of boiling water. Cover and leave to soak for 15–20 minutes, until all the water has been absorbed.

2. Meanwhile, place the clementine slices, pomegranate seeds and chopped herbs in a mixing bowl.

3. Fluff up the bulgur grains with a fork and add to the bowl. Season well and toss to combine. Serve at room temperature.

> **Pomegranates**
> Red, jewel-like pomegranate seeds provide a burst of sweet flavour and are a favourite ingredient in savoury Middle Eastern dishes, such as this Tabbouleh with Pomegranate, Clementine and Parsley. Often described as a 'superfood' because they are high in antioxidants, pomegranates also make delicious desserts, such as Pomegranate and Lime Granita (page 180).

vanilla
pannacotta

Pannacotta is usually made with cream and milk, but we've made a lighter version by replacing these ingredients with yogurt.

SERVES 4

WORTH THE EFFORT

Syns per serving
Original: Free
Green: Free

Preparation time 15 minutes
plus chilling

200g/7oz Quark soft cheese
5 tbsp artificial sweetener
1 tsp vanilla extract
2 x 200g pots Müllerlight vanilla yogurt
1 x 10g sachet gelatine
1 egg white

To garnish
mint leaves

1. Whisk the Quark, sweetener, vanilla extract and yogurt in a bowl until smooth.

2. Place 2 tbsp hot water in a small, heatproof bowl and sprinkle with the gelatine. Stand the bowl in a saucepan of hot water and stir until the gelatine has dissolved. Cool slightly, then whisk into the yogurt mixture.

3. Beat the egg white until softly peaked. Gently fold through the yogurt mixture, then spoon into 4 individual moulds. Chill in the fridge for 3–4 hours until set.

4. When ready, dip the moulds in hot water for a few seconds, then unmould onto individual plates. Garnish with mint leaves and serve.

coffee, chocolate and cognac mousse

Adding brandy to this light and fluffy chocolate mousse gives it a grown-up twist. Strictly for adults only!

SERVES 4

WORTH THE EFFORT

Syns per serving

Original: 3½

Green: 3½

Preparation time 20 minutes plus chilling

100ml/3½fl oz boiling hot black coffee

1 x 10g sachet gelatine

4 sachets Cadbury Highlights Hot Chocolate Drink

3–4 tbsp artificial sweetener

1 tbsp cognac

500g/1lb 2oz very low fat natural fromage frais

2 egg whites

To garnish

very low fat natural fromage frais

8 chocolate-covered coffee beans

mint leaves (optional)

1. Place the hot coffee in a bowl and sprinkle over the gelatine. Stir to dissolve, then set aside to cool slightly.

2. Place the chocolate drink and sweetener in a bowl and whisk in the cognac and fromage frais. Add the coffee mixture and stir well to combine.

3. Whisk the egg whites until softly peaked, then fold into the chocolate mixture with a metal spoon. Divide this mixture between 4 large dessert glasses and chill in the fridge for 3–4 hours, or until set.

4. To serve, place a spoonful of fromage frais on top of each mousse and garnish with the chocolate-covered coffee beans and mint leaves, if using.

pomegranate and lime granita

Pomegranates were once hard to find, but since they've been hailed as a great antioxidant, they're now available in many stores.

SERVES 4 Ⓥ ❋

EASY

Syns per serving

Original: 3

Green: 3

Preparation time 10 minutes plus freezing

600ml/24fl oz pomegranate juice

2 tsp finely grated lime zest

4–5 tbsp artificial sweetener

To garnish

thin wedges of lime

1. Place the pomegranate juice and lime zest in a shallow, freezerproof container, add the sweetener and stir until dissolved. Cover and freeze for 2 hours, or until the mixture starts to look mushy.

2. Using a fork, break up the ice crystals and finely mash. Return the mixture to the freezer for another 2 hours, mashing every 30 minutes, until the ice becomes fine, even crystals.

3. After the final mashing, return the granita to the freezer for at least an hour before serving. Garnish with the lime wedges.

food
optimising
the power to change your life

Although this book is called Slimming World's *Four Seasons Cookbook*, you won't find us recommending a 'slimming diet' anywhere. That's because our weight-loss system, Food Optimising, is not a 'diet' – if by that we mean a temporary measure to lose weight, or a quick fix that we stick to for as long as we can stand it.

And Food Optimising is totally different from the 'diets' that come and go like shooting stars in the media, generating a burst of publicity for their authors and a trail of disappointed slimmers in their wake.

For nearly 40 years now, Food Optimising has been proving its power and effectiveness as a healthy eating plan for life. While it's been refined and developed in that time to reflect social changes and scientific progress, it has stayed true to its principles since it was first launched by Margaret Miles-Bramwell, Slimming World's founder, in 1969.

What set Food Optimising apart then, and continues to do so today, is the way that it turns conventional 'dieting' wisdom on its head. Instead of asking slimmers to eat less, Food Optimising encourages them to eat more. Instead of restrictive diet sheets, there are hundreds of choices and thousands of exciting meals to make using favourite foods. Instead of rules on which foods can be eaten at which times and in which combinations, there is complete freedom.

The idea that those with a weight problem should be urged to enjoy food and eat to satisfy their appetite still comes as a huge shock to some people – especially to many overweight people, who may have spent years believing that they are bad, lazy and unworthy just because they struggle with their weight.

In a society where overweight people are often viewed as patients to be treated or problems to be managed, Slimming World offers a gloriously liberating alternative: an eating plan that offers safe, effective weight loss without huge sacrifice or social isolation, and group support that raises members' self-esteem and empowers them to make the changes they want to see in their lives.

It's a formula that has helped millions of slimmers over the years, and made Slimming World the UK's leading weight management organisation, with over 5,500 groups meeting each week, caring for around 250,000 members.

How does Food Optimising achieve such phenomenal results? How can members lose weight when they are encouraged to eat as much they want, whenever they want? Isn't that how they gained weight in the first place?

One answer to these questions lies in Food Optimising's unique effectiveness as an eating plan. Basing meals on Free Foods, with no measuring, counting or weighing, Food Optimisers quickly lose the fear of hunger and

deprivation that dooms restrictive diets to failure before they start. Free of this anxiety, they begin to relax around food and to understand that they can enjoy eating without feeling guilty. Yet the slimming-friendly qualities of Free Foods ensure that members easily and naturally consume less energy than their bodies require, which is, of course, the key to losing weight. (See pages 186–7 for more on Free Foods.)

Alongside Free Foods, which are its cornerstone, Food Optimising allows slimmers to make daily choices from two further groups of foods: Healthy Extras and Syns (pages 188–9). These ensure that members enjoy a healthy, balanced diet while still being able to choose their favourite foods; but there are limits on both groups, as another way of setting a natural ceiling on the overall energy intake and to keep those weight losses going.

More than this, though, Food Optimising is based on a deep trust and confidence that when people are treated as competent, intelligent adults, they will respond and behave accordingly. Treated like naughty schoolchildren,

with arbitrary rules and petty restrictions, it's human nature to rebel – either openly by eating unwisely, or inwardly by becoming resentful, angry and depressed.

By balancing so much freedom with a light touch of control on Healthy Extras and Syns, Food Optimising liberates slimmers from the need to follow strict rules or to rebel: they are freed from the 'diet' mantra of 'Dare I Eat That?' and from the fear of going hungry or feeling deprived. Instead, Food Optimisers can focus positively on making the changes they want to make to the way they shop, cook and eat, confident that each step takes them nearer to their goal, and knowing they have the support of their group and their Consultant.

In place of the iron willpower that so many restrictive weight-loss plans require, Food Optimising offers choice power. There is no 'one style suits all' approach at Slimming World. Depending on what kinds of foods they like to eat, and how they like to plan their meals, members can take their pick of four 'choices': Green, Original, Mix2Max or Success Express.

And they needn't stick to one choice forever, or even for a week: it's easy to switch between the different options as they're all designed to provide delicious meals and fabulous weight losses. For more on Food Optimising choices, see page 186.

By deciding which choice they want to follow, and picking their Free Foods, Healthy Extras and Syns every day, Slimming World members are in the driving seat of their success from day one. And because they are strengthening their 'choice muscles' week by week instead of relying on someone else's rules, Food Optimisers become confident that they can eat healthily and manage their weight not just for their holiday or after Christmas, but permanently and no matter what is happening in their life.

This is essential, because while most of us could stick to almost any regime for a week or so, the test comes when real life gets in the way. Food Optimising is firmly based on planet Earth, where people work, have families, go to parties, and have 'good days' and 'not so good days'. By using choice power, Slimming World members discover that Food Optimising is generous and flexible enough to cope with any eventuality, and, more importantly, so can they! There is no need to eat separately from the family, avoid meals out and parties, or feel self-conscious about 'being on a diet' when everyone else is enjoying themselves: Food Optimising fits in with each individual's lifestyle, not the other way round.

I feel like shouting from the rooftops!

Police officer Jackie Showers, 43, lost 6st in a year at Jackie Madden's Slimming World group in Riccall, Yorkshire. Jackie, who's 5ft 6in tall and is now a trim 10st 6lb, lives with her husband David and three grown-up stepdaughters.

'When David and I got together ten years ago I relished the chance to indulge my love of cooking, creating meals for him and my three gorgeous stepdaughters. My cooking style wasn't great for my figure, though! I began to put on weight, and as my size went up, my confidence began to slide.

'Joining Slimming World, and realising that I could still cook delicious meals, such as pork patties with coriander and chilli tiger prawns – even David's favourite beef stew and dumplings – was a revelation. And Food Optimising fits in really well with working shifts. I take sandwiches, such as salmon and prawns on wholemeal bread, or a cold Cajun chicken salad, and if I'm working late, I always have lots of fresh fruit handy.

'When I think about some of the diets I've tried in the past, there's no comparison to Food Optimising. David lost a stone without even trying, and I feel like shouting

from the rooftops: "We eat so well! And so much!" Silly, I know, but it reflects how I feel: completely re-energised and alive.'

- **Original choice:** Are your favourite meals a full English breakfast, a traditional roast dinner or a juicy steak? Then Food Optimising's Original choice is for you. Eat your fill of lean, satisfying, protein-rich foods, including beef, chicken, lamb, bacon, turkey, fish and seafood, as well as many other Free Foods, such as all fresh fruit and nearly all vegetables, eggs and dairy products, such as very low fat natural yogurt or fromage frais. Add daily servings of Healthy Extras, such as wholemeal bread, potatoes, high-fibre breakfast cereals and cheese or milk, to provide even more energy, fibre, vitamins and minerals, then choose your Syns for the day – if you have room!

- **Green choice:** Huge plates of pasta, fluffy jacket potatoes, vegetable chilli with a pile of rice … if carbohydrate-rich comfort food is your thing, then Food Optimising's Green choice is for you. Even on your hungriest days, you can satisfy your appetite with potatoes, pasta, rice, couscous and pulses – all are Free Foods on Green – along with all fresh fruit and vegetables, eggs and some dairy products, such as very low fat natural yogurt or fromage frais. Add delicious daily Healthy Extras, such as lean meat or fish, wholemeal bread, high-fibre cereals and cheese or milk to supply even more fibre, vitamins and minerals, then decide how to use your Syns for the day.

- **Mix2Max:** Ideal for people who prefer not to plan too far ahead, Mix2Max allows you to decide whether to go Green or Original at each meal. So if you'd like a full English for breakfast, pasta and tomato sauce for lunch, and a roast chicken dinner in the evening – go for it! Healthy Extras and Syns are still on the menu, so you won't miss out on any nutrients, filling power or your favourite snacks. Mix2Max can be a life-saver if you eat out a lot for work, or some-times have last-minute changes of plan (which most of us do at some time or other). Once you're comfortable with the Green and Original choices, try Mix2Max for a refreshing change.

- **Success Express:** As its name suggests, Success Express is a streamlined Food Optimising choice, excellent for giving your weight loss a boost at those times when you want to focus on results – without going hungry of course! With Success Express, meals are based on Superfree and Free Foods; there's no weighing or measuring, as you fill your plate on a two-thirds Superfree, one-third Free principle. It's still a generous, flexible plan, and it works in a slightly different way from other choices, which is why it's more of a specialist choice. Many members report great results with Success Express once they're familiar with the Green and Original choices.

- **Free2Go:** Designed especially for younger members, Free2Go is a 'super-liberated' choice that guides teenagers to eat more healthily without having to count, weigh or measure any foods, and without worrying about the 'diet' issue. With Free2Go, Food Optimisers fill up on unlimited Green and Original Free Foods, a long list of Healthy Extra choices (most in unlimited quantities), and have a small number of high-fat or high-sugar choices each day. The emphasis is on making 'cool swaps' towards healthier foods. For more on Slimming World's service to teenagers see pages 194–5.

free foods

If Food Optimising is the eating plan that turns conventional dieting wisdom on its head, then Free Foods are the weapons that make Food Optimising so incredibly satisfying, generous, tasty and effective.

Free Foods are the way that slimmers can liberate themselves from a diet sheet, and eat to satisfy their appetite. Free Foods ensure that there is never a danger of running out of your food allowance for the day. And Free Foods mean that slimmers can graze all day, or go back for second or third helpings at meals, exactly as they wish, without compromising their weight-loss success.

For many new members who have previously tried calorie-counting or other restrictive diets, it can be almost overwhelming to read through their Food Optimising guide and find that they are encouraged to eat as much as they like from a huge variety of Free Foods, including things that appear on many a diet's 'banned' list, such as bacon and eggs, baked beans, pasta, potatoes and bananas.

Understandably, some are sceptical and are determined to test Free Foods to their limit, only to find the next week that they have lost weight by eating more than they were previously.

It may feel like magic, but the concept of Free Foods is based on detailed research into the nature of appetite and how it is satisfied. Studies have found that protein-rich foods, such as lean meat and fish, and starchy foods, such as pasta and potatoes, are more satiating – in other words, have more filling power – than foods that are high in fat or sugar.

And at the same time research has established that foods that are low in energy density – which is to say that they are lower in calories, weight for weight, compared to other foods – are also valuable for slimmers because they are filling without piling on the calories. Again, protein-rich foods, such as lean meat and fish, and carbohydrate-rich foods, such as pasta and potatoes, are relatively low in energy density compared to other food groups, such as alcohol and fats. Most fruit and vegetables, and some high-fibre foods, are also low in energy density because they are bulky, watery or both. All of these foods are on the Free Foods list.

Some Free Foods are even lower in energy density than others of their type, and at Slimming World these are known as Speed Foods. While no individual food can be said to be 'fattening' or 'slimming', including plenty of Speed Foods in meals can often help weight loss along.

These key properties of Free Foods explain why they are so effective in enabling Food Optimisers eat as much of them as they like, while naturally limiting their overall energy intake.

Free Foods also generally take time to chew and eat, activating all the signals the body sends to the brain to indicate that the stomach is full. Think how long it takes to eat a jacket potato compared to a packet of crisps: the much more energy-dense crisps quickly disappear and often leave us wanting more.

Some foods, such as all fresh and frozen fruit, most vegetables, eggs, some very low fat dairy products and vegetable proteins, such as Quorn and tofu, are Free on the Green and Original choices, so are known as Superfree Foods. This is useful to know because Superfree snacks, such as a vegetable frittata or a fresh fruit salad, are great to have on hand without having to think whether you're having a Green or Original day. Superfree Foods are also the basis for meals on the Success Express choice (page 185).

Basing meals on Free Foods is good news for general health as well as for weight loss. For example, healthy eating guidelines recommend that we eat at least five portions of fruit and vegetables a day; Food Optimisers, though, are encouraged to eat as many servings as they like – no limits. And Free Foods are generally unprocessed fresh foods, naturally low in fat, salt, sugar and artificial additives – exactly what's recommended for a healthy, well-balanced diet.

small change, big difference

Susan Mackey, 43, is a computer software developer and lives in Gateshead, Tyne & Wear, with her husband Billy and their two teenage daughters. Susan, who's 5ft 9in, lost 3st 9lb in 14 months at Marion Oxley's Slimming World group in Leam Lane, Gateshead, and is now a slim 11st 4lb.

'I used to think that losing weight involved changing your lifestyle completely, or not eating what you wanted to eat, but the brilliant thing about Slimming World was that all I had to do was adjust my normal eating – a small change that made such a big difference!

'For someone with a very busy lifestyle like mine, it couldn't have been more hassle-free. We still have the same dishes we used to, such as steak or fish with vegetables, but without all the oil.

'Eating out isn't a problem either. If I go out for lunch at work, I order a tomato-based pasta sauce instead of a cheesy pasta bake, or I'll go for boiled rice and vegetable dishes if we are having an Indian or Chinese meal. And I still have my favourite latte in a city centre coffee bar!

'The combination of healthier meals and fewer takeaways means that Billy has lost weight too, and my daughter Georgia decided to join Slimming World with me as she wanted to lose a few pounds. I didn't mind at all as I know that she's eating really healthily and isn't depriving herself of anything.'

healthy
extras

Healthy eating guidelines currently recommend that we have a balance in our diet between all the different food groups – starchy foods, fruit and vegetables, dairy produce, meat and fish, and a limited amount of fats and sugary foods.

When you're Food Optimising, Healthy Extras are the way to ensure you get that balance every day, as well as all the fibre, vitamins and minerals needed for optimum health, especially calcium. Calcium is essential for strong bones and teeth, and helps nerves, muscles and blood to function properly. Research has also found that calcium might play a role in weight loss by altering the way in which fat cells function, so keeping a high calcium intake is potentially extra beneficial for slimmers. Members who cannot eat dairy products can choose soya-based alternatives instead.

Unlike Free Foods, Healthy Extras are eaten in measured portions, partly to help control overall energy intake, and partly because some Healthy Extra foods – such as bread, cheese and olive oil – are easy to over-consume.

Each day Food Optimisers choose three or four times from a long list of Healthy Extras. Some Healthy Extras are common to the Green and Original choices: these include dairy products, such as milk and cheese, high-fibre bread and breakfast cereals, dried and canned fruit, and olive oil.

On the Green choice, Healthy Extras also include lean meat and fish, and on the Original choice, they include wholemeal pasta, potatoes, pulses and beans.

As well as being nutritious and tasty, Healthy Extras also make Food Optimising even more flexible and convenient. For instance, if you'd like a chicken sandwich for lunch and a jacket potato with your steak supper on an Original day, or a bacon roll for breakfast and Parmesan cheese on your risotto on a Green day, then your Healthy Extra choices take care of it.

Healthy Extras are also the clear proof that Food Optimising could never be confused with faddy regimes, such as food combining or the Atkins Diet; with plans that separate out different food groups, or are very low in carbohydrates, you would never be able to enjoy spaghetti bolognese, chilli con carne or even good old bangers and mash – all of which are among Food Optimisers' favourites!

syns

We all know that we 'shouldn't' eat too many fatty, sugary foods, or drink too much alcohol, but we also know how counter-productive it can be to deny ourselves completely. That's where Syns come in – a bit like the oil that helps the whole engine run smoothly, Syns are the ingredient that make Food Optimising a realistic, enjoyable healthy eating plan for life.

'Syn' is short for 'synergy', the word that describes what happens when the combined effect of individual elements is more powerful than they would be on their own. There's nothing 'sinful' about Syns! Far from it: Syns are the safety net that takes the guilt out of enjoying a chocolate bar, a glass of wine or a packet of crisps; and having Syns ensures you needn't miss out on little extras, such as mayo in your sandwich or pepper sauce on your steak.

When you're Food Optimising, every food that isn't Free or a Healthy Extra has a Syn value. Each day, Slimming World members can choose how many Syns they would like to use and how to use them. The number of Syns a member has each day can vary, but the average is around 10; as an example, a small glass of wine has 5 Syns, and a small packet of crisps has 6 or 7 Syns.

As we've already seen, Free Foods tend to be basic, unprocessed foods, such as fruit and vegetables, meat and fish, eggs, pasta and rice. By contrast, most processed foods have Syns; these include many ready meals, pies, desserts and fast foods, as well as 'treats' such as chocolate, crisps, cake and alcohol. So keeping an eye on your Syns is another way in which Food Optimising means that you naturally eat more fresh, basic foods and fewer processed foods – which benefits your weight loss, your overall health and your pocket!

Some Slimming World members find that they are so satisfied with their Free Foods and Healthy Extras that they don't feel the need for Syns. This is absolutely their choice, as using the Syns allowance isn't essential for health. Most Food Optimisers, though, find that having Syns gives them just the right balance of freewheeling and control so that they keep on an even keel with their eating and avoid that feeling of having 'blown it' if they break self-imposed rules that are too strict for comfort.

That said, almost all of us have times – maybe a special occasion, or just a really difficult day – when even a generous Syns allowance isn't enough! If you're following a typically restrictive diet, this can spell disaster, either because the 'I've blown it' feeling becomes overwhelming, or because the deprivation of missing out on all the fun becomes unbearable. Needless to say, Slimming World understands this only too well and has a strategy to help members sail through all kinds of testing situations. Ask your group Consultant for more details.

group
support

At Slimming World, group support feels relaxed and fun, yet it's based on a deep understanding of the psychology of slimming. Research shows that joining a group is more effective than going it alone when we aim to make lifestyle changes, but the wrong sort of group culture – one of blame, humiliation or browbeating tactics – can do far more harm than good.

That's why, in addition to their natural warmth and empathy towards slimmers, based on their own experience, Consultants receive state-of-the-art training in supporting, motivating and empowering their members to have confidence in their own judgement and potential.

Far more effective than handing down advice or giving lectures, the power of Slimming World's group support lies in raising members' awareness that they each know best what works for them, and puts them firmly in the driving seat of their success. You're in control of every step on your Slimming World journey, from setting your own target weight (or not, if you'd prefer not to straight away), to deciding each day and each week what you'd like to eat. And at every step your Consultant and fellow members are there to praise your successes, help you smile if the going is a bit tough, and cheer you to the rafters when you reach your target weight.

Slimming World members often join a group feeling that they have nothing left to lose; yet the infectious mix of team spirit, laughter and support ensures that they begin to feel like a winner – a feeling that carries them through to achieve what they thought was impossible.

Group support: FAQs

Q Will the whole group know my weight?
A No, not unless you want them to; the weekly weigh-in is private and confidential. Your Consultant may refer to how much you've lost that week or since you joined, but any other information you share is up to you.

Q Do I have to take part in the group discussion?
A No, you don't have to stay for the whole meeting, or take an active part in it if you'd rather not. But the overwhelming majority of successful members tell us that staying each week and sharing with the group made all the difference between success and failure.

Q Will I have to 'confess' if I've had a bad week?
A What for? It's not a crime! You don't need punishment or forgiveness, just praise for coming to the group even if you weren't looking forward to it, and encouragement to believe that you can easily put any setbacks behind you and confidently take your next step to success.

everyone was so
welcoming

Slimming World's Man of the Year 2007, Peter Tokes, had always been big, but things really got out of hand after he had an accident in 2002. Spinal nerve damage and severe arthritis left Peter on crutches, virtually immobile and feeling very low.

'My weight rocketed,' says Peter. 'The more I put on, the unhappier I became, and the more I relied on comfort foods. Before long I'd gone up to almost 20st.

'I'd heard of Slimming World from a friend's wife, who was a member. But thinking about joining was one thing – actually doing it was another. Then one day Lesley, my wife, put her coat on and said, "Right, get ready – we're going to Slimming World."

'I was very apprehensive – "If it's full of old ladies," I said, "I'm straight out of there" – and tripping over my crutches so that I literally fell through the door didn't exactly help either!

'But from the moment I made my rather embarrassing entrance, everyone was so welcoming. Our Consultant Wendy was warm and friendly, and explained how Food Optimising worked really well, and Kath Johnson, the lovely welcome lady, was equally inspiring. She told me all about her own weight-loss journey and I was immediately hooked.

'I absolutely love Image Therapy: we all help and inspire each other – it's what keeps you going. In fact, now that Lesley's become a Consultant too (she's lost a stone and dropped two dress sizes), I go to meetings three times a week! I collect the money for her and am determined to support her 200 per cent – just as she's supported me.'

body magic

everyday activity for long-term health

Most of us know that being fit is good for our health in all sorts of ways, but knowing it and doing something about it are two different things! It's worth recapping, though, that being active on a regular basis can reduce your risk of developing serious illnesses, help you beat stress and sleep better, tone your body and lift your mood – and that's just for starters.

At Slimming World we understand that it takes more than good intentions to become more active, which is where Body Magic comes in. Forget wearing leotards or jumping up and down to music – unless that's your favourite form of exercise, you don't have to do it. Instead, Body Magic is about building brisk activity into your everyday life in any way you choose, from walking to vigorous housework, from swimming to a kickabout in the garden.

Each week, log your progress along the 'activity pathway' from sedentary to fit, and enjoy your reward of praise from your group as you reach each of these Body Magic awards:

Body Magic: FAQs

Q How much exercise will I have to do?
A Only as much as you want to – none if you don't – as taking part in Body Magic is not compulsory. If you do decide you'd like to mark your progress with Body Magic awards, you start at the level and pace that are comfortable for you, depending on how fit and active you are already.

Q How long do I have to achieve each Body Magic award?
A As long as you like! Experts agree that it's far better for your long-term health to build activity into your life gradually rather than rush into it and risk getting injured or overtired. You can achieve each award at your own pace, and maintain each stage until you feel you're ready to move up to the next.

Q If I take part in Body Magic, can I eat more?
A Food Optimising is already so generous that members find they have no trouble satisfying their appetite, no matter how much exercise they do! However, there is clear evidence that increasing your activity, as well as eating healthily, is a very effective way to optimise your weight loss, so combining Food Optimising with Body Magic is a speedier route to success.

- **Bronze**, when you're active for at least 45 minutes each week, spread over at least three days and maintained for four weeks or more.
- **Silver**, which you reach four weeks after building up to six 15-minute sessions of activity each week, spread over three to five days.
- **Gold**, achieved when you are being active for ten 15-minute sessions a week, spread over five days and maintained for eight weeks. This is the level the government recommends for maintaining good health.
- **Platinum**, when exercise and activity are as automatic and regular as cleaning your teeth and you can't imagine life without them.

Becoming more active helps you burn energy and build muscle, which in turn helps you burn energy more effectively – a win-win result for your weight loss too! And with *Body Magic*, you're in control from the word go: another way in which Slimming World creates the conditions for success to feel natural and inevitable.

life is so much more
rewarding

Parish council manager Nick Riseley, 37, lives in Milton Keynes, Buckinghamshire, with his wife Louise, 32. He lost 4st 3lb at Karen Matthews' Neath Hill Slimming World group in Milton Keynes, and now weighs 13st 3lb.

'My problem first started when I became a musician in the army at the age of 19. That was partly as a result of the socialising that went on, and by the time I left the services a decade later I'd put on an extra 3st. I then met Louise and we married in May 2004. We both worked long and unusual hours, so takeaways and junk food became routine. At my heaviest I was 18st 7lb. Eventually, Louise suggested I try Slimming World, so in April 2005 I joined a group. I really couldn't make sense of the fact that I could eat a huge bowl of pasta or even a whole chicken and still expect to lose weight. However, a month later, I'd lost a stone. After ten weeks it was 2st, and when I played my regular round of golf I found I was no longer puffed out halfway through. By December I'd lost more than 3st and I started going to the gym regularly. I really enjoy the feeling that I'm making progress.

'I still love my food and wine, but life is so much more rewarding when you're a healthy weight. There's nothing you can't do when you are Food Optimising, but plenty more you can do because you are.'

a family approach
forming helpful habits for life

One of the saddest aspects of the 'obesity epidemic' is that it is no longer just an adults' problem. The latest survey shows that within the 11–15 age bracket in England in 2004 some 24 per cent of boys and 26 per cent of girls were obese – twice as many as there were in 1994.

Everyone seems to agree that young people are eating less healthily and being less active than previous generations, yet concerned parents often feel isolated in trying to find not just practical help for their families, but also an understanding of the pressures that they and their children face. The management of weight problems in the young is such a sensitive issue that organisations and official bodies have in the past been reluctant to tackle it.

Since Slimming World began in 1969, we have built up unrivalled experience in supporting individuals as they transform their lives, and research tells us that many Food Optimisers play a powerful, positive role in influencing their family and friends to eat more healthily and become more active.

Slimming World already offers special membership packages for senior citizens, groups of adults and students, and in 2006 we felt it was the right thing to do to offer direct help to younger members of the family, as well as adults, with our groundbreaking Family Affair scheme.

Family Affair offers all the warmth, help and support of a Slimming World group free of charge to those aged 11–15, as long as they attend with a fee-paying parent or guardian and have their GP's written consent to do so. Teenagers even have their own eating plan, Free2Go, a 'super-relaxed' form of Food Optimising, with the emphasis on filling up with nutritious, tasty Free Foods and Healthy Extras, and choosing these instead of foods high in fat and sugar. (See page 185 for more information about Free2Go.)

Within their group, teens and their families discover all kinds of ways to make easy changes in eating, food shopping and lifestyle. Central to Food Optimising, of course, is using plenty of fresh, basic Free Foods to create meals that the whole family can enjoy, with the valuable bonus of getting everyone back around the table to share a meal and enjoy some precious quality time. There is no question of teenagers being 'on a diet', and as Food Optimising fits into young people's lives just as easily as their parents', they needn't fear being marked out as 'different' at school or when out with their friends.

At Slimming World we are very proud of our youngest members and how many thousands of them are finding the courage and commitment to change their lives with the support of their Consultant, fellow members and their families.

A family approach: FAQs

Q **Will my child have to be weighed?**
A Only if he or she wants to be. For 11–15s the focus is firmly on eating more healthily and being more active, not on weight loss. Lots of praise and encouragement is given for every step your child takes towards a healthier lifestyle.

Q **I don't want to lose weight, but I'm worried about my 14-year-old. Can he join on his own?**
A We passionately believe that the best way to help children lead healthier lives is for the person who's mainly responsible for their meals to be involved, so we aren't able to welcome unaccompanied under-16s. If you come with your son, but choose not to join yourself, he will receive our support free of charge, and we ask you to pay a reduced weekly fee. So often, we've found, it's the small changes that parents implement in shopping and cooking that can make such a difference to the whole family's weight and long-term health.

Q **Can I join Slimming World to lose my post-baby weight?**
A Yes, absolutely, once you've had your six-week post-natal check-up. Let your Consultant know if you are breastfeeding so that she can advise you on Food Optimising at this special time.

Caroline Stocks regarded food as her enemy when she was a teenager. 'I want my children to grow up having a healthy relationship with food. Eating Free Foods means that we snack on as much fruit and things like carrot sticks as we want, so the children don't want sweets and chocolates when they're hungry. I never tell them to wait until they have their lunch, and they never have to finish everything on their plate. They're eating the way I'm eating, so they're learning healthy habits alongside me.'

your good health

feel great and take years off!

These days we read a lot about how much money obesity costs the National Health Service, and how overweight people are at greater risk of all kinds of illnesses and disabilities than slim people.

Looking at it another way, though, the great news is that if you are overweight, the health benefits of slimming increase with every pound you lose; many Slimming World members find they see dramatic changes in their health, energy and mobility.

Some of the key benefits of losing excess weight are:

- Reducing raised blood pressure and lowering cholesterol levels, so you need less medication and lower your risk of suffering heart disease and stroke.
- Reducing the risk of developing type 2 diabetes, and helping you control the condition better if you already have it.
- Reducing the strain on joints, resulting in fewer aches and pains and more ease of movement.
- Improving asthma; you may find you need less medication and can breathe more easily.

What's more, the benefits start to have a noticeable effect if you lose just 10 per cent of your starting weight and keep that weight off – an achievement that Slimming World recognises by giving a 'Club 10' award to members who maintain their 10 per cent

weight loss, or go on to lose even more, for ten weeks.

Since many people's first port of call for help is their GP, Slimming World offers Slimming World on Referral through medical practices and health centres. GPs taking part in the scheme can refer patients to Slimming World groups, offering them free membership for 12 weeks. The cost is paid by the GP's practice and is subsidised by Slimming World, but when members join the group they are welcomed just like any other new member, and not marked out as 'different'.

After 12 weeks, patients may ask to be referred again, although many choose to pay for themselves because they're enjoying things so much and losing weight so well. Launched in 2003, Slimming World on Referral is proving popular with GPs and patients alike, offering a practical, low-cost alternative to weight-loss medication and surgery.

Your good health: FAQs

Q I have been prescribed weight-loss medication by my GP. Would it benefit me to join Slimming World?

A Food Optimising is in line with the healthy diet recommended for weight-loss medication patients, so there is no reason why you shouldn't Food Optimise while taking the medication. In addition, our group support and Body Magic programme are great ways to keep your motivation and commitment high as you tackle your weight.

Q I have food intolerances. Can I still Food Optimise?

A Yes, absolutely! Food Optimising is so generous and flexible that you can easily fit it in with any special dietary needs, whether these are related to a medical condition, a religious belief, or simply a dislike of certain foods. With Food Optimising, no foods are banned and none are compulsory.

Q Can you lose weight too quickly with Slimming World?

A Rapid weight loss through crash dieting isn't advisable because the body loses lean tissue as well as fat, which in turn reduces muscle mass and can lower the metabolic rate. Extreme 'yo-yo dieting' is also a bad idea because it sets up a cycle of failure and despair that is damaging to self-esteem. People who have a lot of weight to lose often find that they lose several pounds in their first week of Food Optimising; this rate of loss may continue for several weeks and is not 'too quick', but perfectly normal and safe. Over time our members find that their weight loss averages out at a steady, healthy 1–2lb a week.

Julie Makin had a run of serious health scares, including being diagnosed with stage one cervical cancer. 'But,' she says, 'the final straw came when I was told that I had type 2 diabetes and the doctor suggested that I lose weight. I discovered that Slimming World actively encourages people with diabetes to join.

'From the start it was obvious that with Food Optimising I'd found an eating plan that suited my diabetes perfectly – the weight simply dropped off. Crucially, I also started doing a lot more exercise. Now I walk 5 miles every day, I swim for 60 minutes once a week and I go to the gym three times a week. I really believe Food Optimising and exercise have worked in tandem to make me the slim, active and energetic person that I am today.'

four seasons
menus

Take a week or two to follow our tasty selection of mouth-watering menus and you'll be able to plan your shopping with confidence. You'll soon discover that not only does Food Optimising work, it's fabulously simple too!

These menus are designed to help you understand the variety of meals that are possible when you start Food Optimising (we've included lots of meals that the whole family will enjoy). You can be sure of plenty of nourishing, satisfying food that will keep you full and healthy, and help you lose weight too! We've included some of the recipes featured in this book.

Here's how to use Food Optimising menus most effectively:

1. Decide whether you wish to have a Green day or an Original day and stick to that choice all day. You can make every day a Green day, or include some Original days too. Within the Green menus we have included meat-free choices that are suitable for vegetarians.
2. Pick one breakfast, one lunch and one dinner from your chosen set.
3. Choose around 10–15 Syns-worth of food from the Syns list on page 206. Some Food Optimisers find that they lose weight best on 5 Syns, others on 20 Syns. On some days, if you are going out for a meal or celebrating, you might find you need to use 30. Generally,

we find 10 Syns a day is a good rule of thumb for effective weight loss.

4. Each day choose twice from the following milk and cheese lists to boost your calcium intake, which is vital for a healthy diet.

MILK

350ml/12fl oz skimmed milk
225ml/8fl oz semi-skimmed milk
175ml/6fl oz whole milk
225ml/8fl oz calcium-enriched soya milk
(sweetened or unsweetened)

CHEESE

25g/1oz Cheddar
25g/1oz Edam
25g/1oz Gouda
40g/1½oz mozzarella
40g/1½oz reduced fat Cheddar/Cheshire
3 Dairylea Original triangles
2 mini Babybel cheeses

On the menus that are given on the following pages – divided into Green days and Original days – check out the foods that are marked in **bold**. These can be eaten freely without any weighing or measuring. Fill up on these foods when you feel peckish. You can also turn to our Free Food list on page 204 and select other Free Foods to enjoy whenever you want, in whatever quantity you want.

Maximise your healthy eating by:

- Eating at least five portions of fresh fruit and vegetables every day. Frozen fruit and frozen and canned vegetables can also be used.
- Trimming all visible fat off meat and removing any skin from poultry.
- Varying your choices as much as possible to ensure you're getting the widest range of nutrients in your diet.
- Eating at least two portions of fish a week, of which one is an oily fish.
- Aiming to keep your salt intake to no more than 6g a day (1 level tsp). As well as limiting the amount of table salt you add to food, watch out for salt added to manufactured foods and sauces. Try flavouring foods with herbs and spices instead.
- Remembering the latest recommendations regarding intake of fluids, which is to aim for 6–8 cups, mugs or glasses of any type of fluid per day, and to vary your choices to include water and low-calorie drinks (sorry, alcohol doesn't count).

Note for Slimming World members: Healthy Extra B choices are built into the menus.

When you've experienced the pleasure of Food Optimising on your plate you'll want to design your own menus. You can do this with the complete Food Optimising system, available at Slimming World groups throughout the UK.

green menus

BREAKFASTS

1. Two Weetabix served with milk from the allowance and topped with plenty of sliced **banana**.

2. Two slices of wholemeal toast topped with heaps of **baked beans**. Follow with a juicy **peach** or two.

3. Fresh **grapefruit** followed by 25g/1oz Triple Berry Shredded Wheat served with milk from the allowance.

4. A large, fluffy **omelette** filled with 25g/1oz grated Cheddar cheese and served with heaps of grilled **mushrooms** and **tomatoes**, followed by any **fresh fruit** of your choice.

5. 25g/1oz Jordans Special Muesli layered with lots of **very low fat natural yogurt** and sliced **strawberries** in a tall glass.

6. Three rashers of grilled lean bacon served with an **egg** fried in Fry Light, and plenty of **baked beans** and grilled **mushrooms**.

7. 25g/1oz Shreddies topped with lots of fresh **raspberries** or **strawberries** and served with milk from the allowance.

8. **Quorn sausages**, any variety, grilled and stuffed into a 50g/2oz wholemeal roll. Nibble on fresh **pineapple** slices while they're cooking.

9. Boiled **eggs** served with 'soldiers' cut from two slices of wholemeal toast. Follow with chunks of **fresh fruit** stirred into a pot of **Müllerlight yogurt**, any variety.

10. **Melon** boat filled with 25g/1oz All-Bran Sultana Bran and drizzled with lots of **very low fat natural fromage frais**.

LUNCHES

*denotes recipe suggestion with picture

1. 110g/4oz chicken breast, grilled or baked, and served with heaps of **new potatoes**, **peas**, **broccoli** and **baby whole sweetcorn**. Follow with a large bowl of **strawberries** smothered in **very low fat natural yogurt**.

2. Two slices of wholemeal bread topped with mountains of **baked beans** and a poached **egg**. Follow with **fresh fruit** of your choice.

3. Lots of cooked **pasta shapes** mixed with 110g/4oz drained tuna canned in brine and plenty of chopped **cucumber**, **tomatoes**, **beetroot** and **spring onion**, drizzled with fat-free vinaigrette. Slice lots of **banana** and stir into a **Müllerlight Toffee Yogurt**.

4. 75g/3oz lean roast beef served with mountains of mashed **potatoes**, dry-roast **potatoes** and **parsnips**, **peas** and **carrots**. Finish with **fresh fruit** of your choice.

5. **Spring Vegetable Soup** (page 16) served with a 50g/2oz crusty wholemeal roll, followed by a bowl of chopped **mango** topped with lashings of **very low fat natural fromage frais**.

6. 150g/5oz cod fillet, grilled or baked, and served with Potato, Fresh Bean and Herb Salad (page 60*) and lots of mixed **salad leaves**. Finish with some **cherries**.

7. Soufléd Jacket Potatoes (page 102*) served with 75g/3oz lean gammon steak, lots of **baked beans** and a huge crisp **salad**. Follow with a few **plums**.

8. Angel Hair Pasta with Chilli and Coriander (page 162*), followed by 350g/12oz pears canned in juice smothered with **Nestlé Sveltesse 0% Fat Yogurt**, any variety.

9. Two slices of wholemeal bread filled with cheese from the allowance and lots of sliced **tomato**, **cucumber**, **onion** and **baby salad leaves**. Finish with a **banana** and an **orange**.

10. Vegetable curry made with lots of **onions**, garlic, **courgettes**, **peppers**, **cauliflower**, **mushrooms**, chopped **tomatoes** and curry powder and served with mountains of boiled **rice**. Follow with 350g/12oz apricots canned in juice.

DINNERS
*denotes recipe suggestion with picture

1. Vegetable stir-fry: **broccoli** and **cauliflower** florets, chopped **carrots**, mixed **peppers**, **spring onions**, **button mushrooms**, **bean sprouts** and **water chestnuts** stir-fried with garlic, herbs and soy sauce served with mountains of **couscous**. Enjoy Ginger Rhubarb and Orange Custard (page 52) for afters.

2. A large **jacket potato** filled with canned **chilli beans in chilli sauce** and served with a huge crisp **salad**. Follow with a large bunch of **grapes**.

3. **Spring Vegetable Risotto** (page 32*). Follow with lots of **fresh fruit** chunks stirred into lashings of **very low fat natural yogurt**.

4. Bolognese sauce made with **Quorn mince**, **onions**, garlic, chopped **tomatoes** and Italian herbs and served on a pile of boiled **spaghetti**. Follow with an **apple** and a **pear** for pud.

5. **Creamy Courgette Linguine with Mint** (page 86*) followed by Vanilla and Gooseberry Fool (page 96).

6. Macaroni and Cauliflower Gratin (page 128*) served with **new potatoes**, **peas** and **carrots** and a crisp mixed **salad**. Follow with slices of fresh **pineapple**.

7. Kedgeree (page 166*), followed by a crunchy **pear** or two.

8. Lots of boiled **pasta** topped with a sauce made from canned **tomatoes** mixed with plenty of chopped **mushrooms**, mixed **peppers**, **onions** and garlic. Raid the **fruit** bowl for afters.

9. **Slimming World Chips** served with heaps of **baked beans** and an **egg** fried in Fry Light. (To make the chips, par-boil chipped potatoes for 5 minutes, then drain and leave for 10 minutes. Transfer to a baking tray, spray with Fry Light and bake at 240°C/Gas 9 for 20–25 minutes.) Finish with a large bowl of chopped **strawberries**, **melon** and **kiwi** smothered in **very low fat natural yogurt**.

10. **Batchelor's Savoury Rice**, any variety, made up as directed and mixed with any cooked, chopped **vegetables** of your choice. Follow with a large bowl of fresh or frozen **berries** smothered in your favourite **Müllerlight yogurt**.

original menus

BREAKFASTS

1. Fresh **orange** and **grapefruit** segments followed by lots of grilled lean **bacon** served with plenty of grilled **mushrooms** and **tomatoes**, poached **eggs** and two slices of wholemeal toast.

2. 25g/1oz All-Bran Bran Flakes topped with lots of sliced **banana** and served with milk from the allowance.

3. A large plain **omelette** served with lots of grilled lean **bacon** and 150g/5oz baked beans, followed with **fresh fruit**.

4. Two slices of wholemeal toast topped with scrambled **egg** mixed with **smoked salmon** and a little chopped dill. Follow with a few fresh **apricots**.

5. Slice a **banana** (or two) lengthways, sprinkle with 25g/1oz Alpen and smother in **very low fat natural yogurt**.

6. Grilled **kippers** served with lots of **tomatoes** and **mushrooms** and two slices of wholemeal toast. Finish with a bowl of **berries** topped with **Nestlé Sveltesse 0% Fat Yogurt**, any variety.

7. 28g/1oz porridge oats made with milk from the allowance and topped with lots of fresh or frozen **berries**.

8. Two slices of wholemeal bread filled with lots of grilled lean **bacon** and an **egg** fried in Fry Light. Follow with a juicy **peach**.

9. Two Weetabix served with milk from the allowance, followed by lots of chopped **strawberries** stirred into a pot of **Müllerlight yogurt**, any variety.

10. Chunks of **fresh fruit** layered in a tall glass with lots of **very low fat natural yogurt** and 25g/1oz Raisin Wheats.

LUNCHES

*denotes recipe suggestion with picture

1. Spanish-style Meatballs (page 78) served with 100g/3½oz (boiled weight) wholemeal spaghetti and a large **mixed salad**. Follow with a juicy **peach** or two.

2. A 50g/2oz wholemeal roll filled with plenty of **prawns** mixed with **very low fat natural fromage frais** and lots of baby **salad leaves**. Follow with **fresh fruit**.

3. Lots of lean roast **lamb** served with mint sauce, 200g/7oz new potatoes in their skins and heaps of **broccoli**, **carrots**, **cabbage** and **baby whole sweetcorn**. Finish with a bowl of **strawberries** smothered in **Müllerlight yogurt**.

4. Lots of grilled lean **bacon** served with 150g/5oz baked beans and plenty of scrambled **egg** and poached **button mushrooms**. Follow with a large bunch of **grapes**.

5. Two slices of wholemeal bread crammed with lean **ham** and lots of sliced **tomato**, **cucumber** and **onion** and mixed baby **salad leaves**. Mix plenty of **fresh fruit** chunks into **very low fat natural yogurt**.

6. An **omelette** filled with 25g/1oz grated Cheddar (from the allowance), served with grilled **tomatoes** and **onion** wedges, and a **crisp salad**. Follow with **melon** slices.

7. Pan-cooked Skate with Bacon (page 36*) served with 200g/7oz new potatoes in their skins and mountains of **baby carrots**, **mangetout** and **green beans**. Enjoy Mango Sorbet for afters (page 55).

8. A large lean **gammon steak** grilled and topped with slices of fresh **pineapple** and served with a 225g/8oz (raw weight) jacket potato and lots of grilled **tomatoes** and **mushrooms** and an **egg** fried in Fry Light. Finish off the **pineapple** for pudding.

9. **Thai Fish Cakes with Cucumber Dipping Sauce** (page 106) served with a 225g/8oz (raw weight) jacket potato and a huge **mixed salad**. Follow with a **fresh fruit** salad smothered in **Nestlé Sveltesse 0% Fat Yogurt**, any variety.

10. Baked Haddock with Tomatoes and Spinach (page 150*) served with heaps of mashed **turnip** or **swede** and any **Free vegetables** of your choice. Follow with a 225g/8oz baked apple filled with 1 level tbsp mincemeat and topped with lashings of **very low fat natural fromage frais**.

DINNER
*denotes recipe suggestion with picture

1. Strips of **beef** stir-fried in Fry Light with freshly chopped herbs and finely chopped chillies, mixed with plenty of **button mushrooms**, **baby carrots**, **mangetout**, **bean sprouts**, mixed **peppers** and **spring onions**. Follow with Coffee, Chocolate and Cognac Mousse (page 179).

2. Lean **pork** steaks, grilled and served with mountains of mashed **swede** and plenty of **cabbage** and **Brussels sprouts**. Finish with a **banana** and an **apple**.

3. Slices of **honeydew melon** followed by a fresh **tuna** steak, chargrilled and served with **asparagus**, **courgettes** and **baby whole sweetcorn**.

4. Grilled **chicken** breast served with plenty of **broccoli**, **cauliflower** and **spinach**. Follow with lots of sliced **banana** stirred into lashings of **very low fat natural yogurt** flavoured with cinnamon.

5. A large grilled lean **steak** topped with plenty of cooked **prawns** and served with lots of **green beans** and **carrots** and a large **mixed salad** tossed in fat-free vinaigrette. Finish with a bowl of **berries** smothered in your favourite **Müllerlight yogurt**.

6. A large **cod** or **haddock** fillet, grilled and served with mountains of roasted vegetables, such as mixed **peppers**, **onion wedges** and **vine tomatoes**. Follow with **fresh fruit** of your choice.

7. Salmon on Wilted Spring Greens (page 40*) served with a large **mixed salad**. Follow with a large bunch of **grapes**.

8. **Grilled Pork Steak with Plum and Mango Salsa** (page 76*) served with plenty of **asparagus**, **cauliflower** and **sugar snap peas**. Finish with slices of fresh **pineapple**.

9. **Lamb and Root Vegetable Casserole** (page 120*) served with additional **Free vegetables**, if you wish. Follow with a Blackberry and Pear Crumble (page 136*).

10. Individual Steak and Kidney Pie (page 156*) served with plenty of **cauliflower**, **broccoli** and **cabbage**. Follow with some **plums**.

free food
selection

We have listed many of our Free Foods here. For the full list, you will need to become a Slimming World member.

KEY TO SYMBOLS

H	=	healthy
HH	=	vital to health
S	=	weight loss boost
SS	=	extra weight loss boost
F	=	extra fibre
FF	=	extra-rich fibre
C	=	good source of calcium
CC	=	very good source of calcium

GREEN CHOICE FREE FOODS

All vegetables are classed as a Free Food when on a Green day.

Grains, Pulses and Vegetables

Bulgur wheat	H		
Couscous	H		
Dried pasta, all types	H		
Polenta	H		
Rice, all types	H		
Baked beans	H	SS	F
Chickpeas	H		F
Lentils	H	S	F
Peas	H	SS	F
Red kidney beans	H	SS	FF
Soya beans	H		FF
Potatoes	HH		
Quorn	H	S	F
Tofu			CC

Dairy

Eggs		
Quark soft cheese	H	C
Very low fat natural cottage cheese	H	C
Very low fat natural fromage frais	H	C

Very low fat natural yogurt	H	C
Müllerlight yogurt		C
Nestlé Sveltesse 0% Fat Yogurt		C
Shape Lasting Satisfaction Yogurt		C

The following fruits can be eaten freely as long as they are fresh or frozen varieties.

Fruit

Apples	HH	S	
Apricots	HH	S	
Bananas	HH		
Blackberries	HH	SS	F
Blueberries	HH		
Cherries	HH	S	
Cranberries	HH	SS	F
Gooseberries	HH	SS	
Grapefruit	HH	SS	
Grapes	HH		
Kiwi fruit	HH	S	
Mango	HH		
Melon	HH	SS	
Nectarines	HH	S	
Oranges	HH	S	
Papaya	HH	S	
Peaches	HH	S	
Pears	HH	S	
Pineapple	HH	S	
Plums	HH	S	
Pomegranates	HH		F
Raspberries	HH	SS	
Rhubarb	HH	SS	
Satsumas	HH	S	
Strawberries	HH	SS	

ORIGINAL CHOICE FREE FOODS

Not all vegetables are Free Foods on the Original Choice.
Choose freely from the following list.

Vegetables

Asparagus	HH	S	
Aubergine	HH	S	
Baby whole sweetcorn	HH	S	
Beans, French/green	HH	S	
Beetroot	HH	S	
Broccoli	HH	S	
Brussels sprouts	HH		F
Cabbage	HH	S	
Carrots	HH	S	
Cauliflower	HH	S	
Celery	HH	S	
Courgettes	HH	S	
Cucumber	HH	S	
Leeks	HH	S	
Mangetout	HH	S	
Mushrooms	HH	S	
Onions	HH	S	
Peppers	HH	S	
Salad leaves	HH	S	
Spinach	HH	S	C
Spring onions	HH	S	
Squash, all types	HH	S	
Sugar snap peas	HH	S	
Swede	HH	S	
Tomatoes	HH	S	
Quorn	H	S	F
Tofu			CC

Poultry

Chicken/Turkey, no fat or skin	H	S

Meat

Bacon/Gammon/Ham/Pork	
Beef	
Lamb	

Fish

Cod/Haddock	H	SS
Halibut	H	S
Kippers	H	
Mackerel (not smoked)	H	
Plaice/Sole	H	SS
Salmon (fresh, canned and smoked)	H	
Tuna, canned in brine	H	S
Tuna, fresh	H	

Shellfish

Crab	H	SS	C
Prawns	H	S	

Dairy

Eggs		
Quark soft cheese	H	C
Very low fat natural cottage cheese	H	C
Very low fat natural fromage frais	H	C
Very low fat natural yogurt	H	C
Müllerlight yogurt		C
Nestlé Sveltesse 0% Fat Yogurt		C
Shape Lasting Satisfaction Yogurt		C

The following fruits can be eaten freely as long as they are
fresh or frozen varieties.

Fruit

Apples/Apricots	HH	S	
Bananas	HH		
Blackberries	HH	SS	F
Blueberries	HH		
Cherries	HH	S	
Cranberries	HH	SS	F
Gooseberries	HH	SS	
Grapefruit	HH	SS	
Grapes	HH		
Kiwi fruit	HH	S	
Mango	HH		
Melon	HH	SS	
Nectarines/Oranges	HH	S	
Papaya/Peaches	HH	S	
Pears	HH	S	
Pineapple	HH	S	
Plums	HH	S	
Pomegranates	HH		F
Raspberries/Rhubarb	HH	SS	
Satsumas	HH	S	
Strawberries	HH	SS	

syns selection

Listed below is a selection of Syn values for foods that you can enjoy every day. You can choose 10–15 Syns each day. The values apply to both the Green and Original choices.

Alcohol and drinks	Syns
1 sachet Highlights/Options Hot Chocolate	2
25ml/1fl oz measure of any spirit	2½
300ml/½pt lemonade/orangeade/shandy	3½
150ml/¼pt glass of wine	5
300ml/½pt beer/lager	5
300ml/½pt cider	5
300ml/½pt cola/root beer	6

Biscuits, each	Syns
Cheese thin/water biscuit	1
Chocolate finger	1½
Fruit shortcake/rich tea	2
Cream cracker/cheese straw	2
Jaffa cake/ginger nut	2½
Custard cream	3
HobNob	3½
Chocolate digestive/jammie dodger	4

Cakes, each	Syns
Mr Kipling French Fancy	5
Cadbury Mini Roll	6
Mr Kipling Country/Lemon Slice	6
Chocolate Cup Cake	7½
Mr Kipling Mini Battenberg	7½
Individual Fruit Pie	10½

Chocolates and sweets, standard bag/tube, etc.	Syns
Milky Bar	3½
Fun-size bars	5
2 finger Kit Kat	5½
Fudge/Milky Way	6
Jellytots/Polo Fruits/Polo Mints	7½
Fruit Gums	8½
Flake	9
Fruit Pastilles/Maltesers	9½

Crisps, standard bag	Syns
French Fries/Golden Lights	4½
Quavers/Ryvita Minis	5
Snack-a-Jacks Butter Toffee Popcorn	7½
Mini Cheddars, Original	9
Walkers Crisps	9½

Desserts, per pot	Syns
Rowntree's Ready to Eat Jelly Pot	5
Cadbury Light Chocolate Mousse (100g pot)	5½
Müllerice, Only 1% Fat	6
Danone Goodies Trifle	7½
Onken Lite Mousse	8

Ice creams/Lollies	Syns
Fruit Pastil Ice Lolly	3
Mini Calippo	3½
50g/2oz scoop low fat ice cream	4
Fab Ice Lolly	4
Solero	5
Strawberry Cornetto	9½

Meal accompaniments, sauces and spreads	Syns
Aerosol cream: 2 level tbsp	½
Jam/marmalade: 1 level tsp	½
Mustard: 1 level tsp	½
Brown sauce/tomato ketchup: 1 level tbsp	1
Custard made with skimmed milk: 2 level tbsp	1
Gravy made without fat: 4 level tbsp	1
Honey, all varieties: 1 level tsp	1
Horseradish sauce: 1 level tbsp	1
Reduced calorie salad cream: 1 level tbsp	1½
Reduced calorie mayonnaise: 1 level tbsp	2½
Margarine/spread, low fat variety: 25g/1oz	5½
Oil, any variety: 1 level tbsp	6

index

index